G000134394

The 'Prince George'
and a hundred other

PLYMOUTH
PUBS
PAST & PRESENT

written and compiled by
CHRIS ROBINSON

edited by Terry Guswell

additional research Doreen Mole

Pen&inK
PUBLISHING

British Library Cataloguing-in-Publication Data
Robinson, Chris, 1954-
   Pubs of Plymouth past and present : the Prince George and a hundred other
   1.Bars (Drinking establishments) - England - Plymouth - History
   2.Bars (Drinking establishments) - England - Plymouth - Pictorial works
   I.Title
   647.9'5'0942358

   ISBN 0951074741

Design: Chris Robinson, Terry Guswell, Rob Warren and Clive Hooper

First Published November 1997

Printed and bound in Great Britain
by Latimer Trend & Company Ltd.
Estover Road
Plymouth PL6 7PY, Devon

Published by
Pen & Ink Publishing
34 New Street
Barbican
Plymouth PL1 2NA, Devon
01752-228120

PLYMOUTH PUBS
PAST & PRESENT

Prince George - Stonehouse - *Closed 1939 later demolished* .... ❑

Archer Inn - Archer Terrace, North Road West .... ❑

Ark Royal - Fore Street, Devonport - *Now Zoo Rooms* .... ❑

Breakwater Inn - Cattedown - *Converted to flats 1997* .... ❑

Britannia - Milehouse .... ❑

Brook Inn - Longbrook Street, Plympton .... ❑

Brown Bear - Chapel Street, Stonehouse .... ❑

Butchers' Arms - Cross Street, Devonport - *Demolished late 1950s* ..... ❑

Casey's - Marlborough Street, Devonport - *Closed in 1997* .... ❑

Chester Cup - Union Street - *Closed 1957* .... ❑

Clarence - Gibbon Street - *Demolished early 1960s* .... ❑

Clarence Hotel - Clarence Place, Stonehouse .... ❑

Clipper - Union Street .... ❑

Commercial Inn - Lambhay Hill, The Barbican .... ❑

Corner House - New George Street .... ❑

Criterion - Union Street - *Closed 1959 and demolished* .... ❑

Crown Hotel - Chapel Street, Devonport .... ❑

Dolphin - The Barbican .... ❑

Falstaff Inn - George Street - *Destroyed 1941* .... ❑

Farmer's Home - Drake Street - *Demolished 1950s* .... ❑

Fawn Hotel - Prospect Street - *Now a private club* .... ❑

Ferry House Inn - Wolseley Road, St. Budeaux .... ❑

First and Last - Exeter Street .... ❑

Frederick Inn - Frederick Street - *Closed 1939* .... ❑

Globe Hotel - Bedford Street - *Demolished 1899* .... ❑

Golden Lion - Fore Street, Devonport - *Destroyed 1941* ...... ❑

Good Companions - Mayflower Street .... ❑

Granby Cellars - Russell Street - *Closed in 1997* .... ❑

Grand Duchess - Gibbon Street .... ❑

Gypsy Tent - Albert Road - *Closed 1936, building still standing* .... ❑

Half Moon - Pembroke Street, Devonport - *Re-launched as cafe 1997*. ❑

Himalaya - Pembroke St., Devonport - *Closed 1954 and demolished* ... ❑

King's Arms - Pembroke Street, Devonport .... ❑

Laira Inn - - *Demolished 1956* .... ❑

Lion and Column - Ham Green .... ❑

Lockyer Tavern - Lockyer Street - *Demolished 1982* .... ☐
Lord Beresford - Cumberland Street .... ☐
Lord High Admiral - Stonehouse Street .... ☐
Mall - Cornwall Street, Plymouth - *Now Pig & Truffle* .... ☐
Maritime - Southside Street, The Barbican .... ☐
Marlborough Hotel - Marlborough St., Devonport - *Demolished 1972* ☐
Masonic Inn - Devonport Road .... ☐
Mayflower Hotel - The Barbican - *Destroyed 1941* .... ☐
Mayflower Inn - Lakeside Drive, Ernesettle .... ☐
Mechanics Inn - George Street, Stonehouse .... ☐
Melbourne Inn - Cecil Street - *Closed in 1997* .... ☐
Newmarket Hotel - Cornwall Street, Devonport - *Destroyed 1941* .... ☐
Newmarket - Market Way .... ☐
Nicholson's - George Street - *Closed 1936* .... ☐
Noah's Ark - Saltash Street - *Destroyed 1941* .... ☐
No Name Inn - Richmond Street - *Closed 1956 and demolished* .... ☐
No Place Inn - North Road West .... ☐
Norley Inn - Ebrington Street - *Demolished late 1960s* .... ☐
Ocean Mail - Millbay Road - *Closed 1956 and demolished* ..... ☐
Oddfellow's Arms - Devonport Road, Stoke .... ☐
Old Chapel - Ker Street, Devonport - *Closed in 1997* .... ☐
Olive Branch - Wyndham Road East - *Now The Library* .... ☐
Passage House Inn - Cattedown - *Demolished 1902 and rebuilt* .... ☐
Pennycomequick - Central Park Avenue .... ☐
Penrose Inn - Penrose Street, North Road West .... ☐
Pheasant Pluckers Arms - Albert Road, Stoke .... ☐
Phoenix Tavern - Phoenix Street .... ☐
Pilgrim's Cafe Bar - The Barbican - *Now Bar PL One* .... ☐
Prince of Wales - Russell Street - *Closed 1951 and demolished* .... ☐
Queen's Arms - Southside Street, The Barbican .... ☐
Queen's Dock - Charlotte Street .... ☐
Queen's Hotel - Union Street - *Demolished late 1980s* .... ☐
Railway Inn - Waterloo Street, Stoke - *Closed in 1997* .... ☐
Richmond Inn - - *Demolished late 1880s* .... ☐
Rising Sun - Marsh Mills - *Closed 1986 and demolished* ..... ☐

Robin Hood Inn - St. Mary Street - *Closed 1961* .... ❏
Rose and Crown - Old Town Street - *Demolished 1920s* .... ❏
Royal Adelaide - Adelaide Street, Devonport .... ❏
Royal Albert Hotel - Martin Terrace - *Destroyed 1941* .... ❏
Royal Marine - Torridge Way, Efford .... ❏
Russell Arms - Russell Street - *Closed 1954 and Demolished*............. ❏
Seymour Arms - Seymour Street .... ❏
Shades Wine Vaults - Queen Street, Plymouth .... ❏
Shakespeare Hotel - Theatre Ope, Devonport .... ❏
Sir Francis Chichester - The Barbican - *Now part of Bar PL One* .... ❏
Sirius Frigate - Pembroke St., Devonport - *Closed 1870s* .... ❏
St. Aubyn Wine & Spirit Vaults - St. Aubyn Street - *Closed 1950s*...... ❏
St. Levan Inn - St. Levan Road, Devonport .... ❏
Standard Inn - Queen Street, Devonport .... ❏
Steam Packet Inn - Cornwall Beach, Devonport .... ❏
Stoke Inn - Devonport Road, Stoke .... ❏
Stoke Vaults - Waterloo Street, Stoke .... ❏
Stonemasons Arms - Albert Road, Devonport............................ ❏
Swallow - Breton Side .... ❏
Swan - Cornwall Beach, Devonport - *Converted to flats 1997* .... ❏
Talbot - Union Street - *Demolished 1980s*................................... ❏
Tamar Inn - Morshead Road - *Demolished 1890s & rebuilt*.............. ❏
Tavistock Hotel - Tavistock Street - *Destroyed 1941* .... ❏
Thistle Park Tavern - Commercial Road, Coxside .... ❏
Two Trees - Fore Street, Devonport - *Destroyed 1941* .... ❏
Valletort Inn - Claremont Street... ❏
Western Hotel - Fore Street, Devonport..................................... ❏
White Lion - Clarence Street, Stonehouse - *Closed 1995, now a cafe*... ❏
White Swan - George Street, Devonport - *Closed 1960s* .... ❏
Woodland Fort Inn - Butt Park Road, Honicknowle .... ❏
Ye Butchers Arms - Tavistock Road - *Closed 1910s & demolished*...... ❏

NB Closed in 1997 means that the pub was closed at time of going to press, it does not preclude the possibility of it re-opening.

ACKNOWLEDGEMENTS

Without the *Evening Herald* providing the weekly opportunity for the series that has spawned this second volume of Plymouth Pubs it is doubtful you would be now reading this and without Terry Guswell, who formats, scans and indexes the whole lot, you certainly would not now be holding this book. So thanks to Rachel Campey and her predecessor as Editor of the *Herald*, Alan Cooper, and to features chief Mike Bramhall and his predecessor Stuart Fraser. Thanks too to Sue for sparing Terry and to Stan for putting up with the fact that Doreen is not yet ready to retire. For two years now Doreen Mole has filed and found all manner of material for this and other projects - thank you.

Similarly Rob Warren my colleague in our New Street operation has made sure that "any other business" has been taken care of, so that projects like this can get off the ground. In much the same way my partner and publisher, Clare Robinson has been a constant source of encouragement both inside and outside many of the pubs here featured.

For the old pubs thanks to Coleen Fry for much of the photographic material, and to County Librarian Alison Shute and Deputy Museum Curator Mark Tosdevin for allowing us to use pictures from their respective collections. Various pictures have also come from the *Evening Herald* and *Western Morning News* library and to them again our grateful thanks.

Hopefully the value of collecting material like this together in one place will be appreciated by many and I must also thank all those individuals who have supplied odd photographs of pubs that we would otherwise have been unable to show you including Joan Dancer and Fred Colton.

When it comes to compiling lists of licensees, the records from the Plymouth Magistrates Court from 1920 onwards are invaluable and invariably more accurate than any other source and thanks to Phil Parsons, Elizabeth Goss, Roseanne Beatson and David Ashby of the licensing department for their help. Prior to 1920 the Street Directories to be found in the Local Studies Library are most useful and the work that the late Henry Horwill contributed, going through the directories for all the Devonport pubs, is particularly helpful. Thanks to Jan Horrell, Ian Criddle, Margaret Willcocks and Malcolm Matthews of the library staff and to Mr Broderick who left to the library perhaps the most remarkable set of records on Devonport ever produced. And finally thanks to the old man, Des Robinson, happy to visit any pub in the line of duty and generally, and generously, usually the first to put his hand in his pocket! Cheers, here's to you all.

Plymouth
October 1997

INTRODUCTION

If ever you needed a simple scale to calculate the economic decline of Devonport consider if you will its pubs. For those who have only known post-war Devonport it may seem hard to believe that there were over a hundred pubs within the scope of this map at the outbreak of war in 1939, today there are barely twenty with a further half a dozen or so currently closed, their fate undecided. At the time of going to press the Half Moon is operating as a cafe, the Swan is being converted to flats, the Gypsy Tent has long since been operating as a shop, while the Standard is being refurbished and is about to re-open after being boarded up for some time. Others boarded up at present are Casey's, the Marquis of Granby, the Lugger, the Cambridge, the Old Chapel and the Prince of Wales (some of them are featured here, the Prince of Wales was in the earlier volume and the Lugger and Cambridge will be in subsequent publications). Earlier this year two other Devonport pubs were re-launched and re-named after a period of closure - the Ark Royal became the very modern Zoo Rooms while the Queen and Constitution is now an Irish bar called Heggarty's.

Clearly many Devonport pubs were victims of the war. A great number were wiped out in 1941, never to be rebuilt, indeed for many rebuilding was simply not an option, as something like fifty of Devonport's pre-war pubs stood on sites swallowed up by the post-war Dockyard extensions. More than thirty of them behind the great grey wall that, in the 1950s, sectioned off most of the town's principal thoroughfares; Fore Street and Cumberland Street, plus St. Aubyn Street, Tavistock Street, Catherine Street, Barrack Street, Market Street and many other smaller roads. At Morice Town there was a similar story as Moon Street, William Street and John Street all found themselves on the wrong side of the wall.

You could perhaps be forgiven for thinking that the loss of all these streets and the pubs that were in them would have meant better chance of survival for those that remained, particularly when the Dockyard was enjoying a certain post-war prosperity itself. However, more recently, Devonport has had to contend with a contracting, rather than expanding Dockyard, certainly in terms of workforce if not in terms of

PAST DEVONPORT PUBS

PRE-WAR DEVONPORT

PRESENT DEVONPORT PUBS

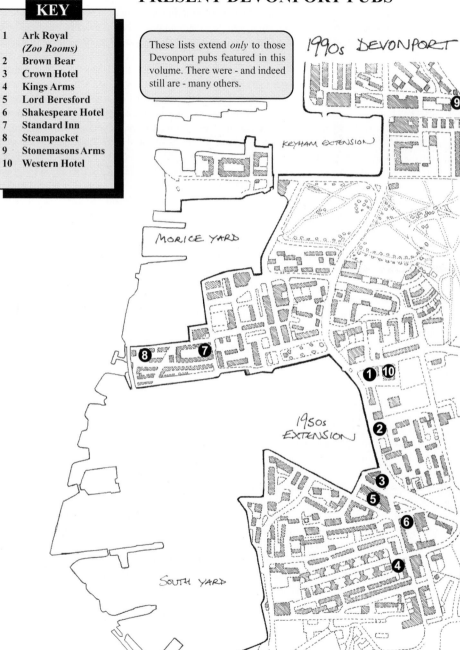

KEY

1 Ark Royal
  (Zoo Rooms)
2 Brown Bear
3 Crown Hotel
4 Kings Arms
5 Lord Beresford
6 Shakespeare Hotel
7 Standard Inn
8 Steampacket
9 Stonemasons Arms
10 Western Hotel

These lists extend *only* to those Devonport pubs featured in this volume. There were - and indeed still are - many others.

1990s DEVONPORT

KEYHAM EXTENSION

MORICE YARD

1950s EXTENSION

SOUTH YARD

acreage. There is even another sense in which the term contracting is appropriate as currently something like 10% of the Dockyard workforce are employed on a contract basis. The number of full-time DML employees is presently in the order of 3,600 - compare that with the 15,000 working there in the late 1930s and you can see the scale of economic decline. In an age when unemployment is already high Plymouth, Devonport has seen it's major employer shed thousands of jobs. Happily, of course, this is partly because the Government no longer feels the need to maintain such a large Navy and across-the-board Defence cuts have had a harsh economic impact on those areas which traditionally relied on the Services. Devonport with its Dockyard and its Army Barracks is one of the country's hardest hit examples. From the very beginning of the Dockyard, in the late seventeenth century, Devonport thrived thanks to the Government's patronage of the place as a naval and military base. Until 1939 war had always brought a certain amount of prosperity to the area and the lack of it and the lack of the threat of it, has always been bad news. Devonport went through a particularly rough patch in the 1820s after the activity that had surrounded the Napoleonic Wars at last subsided. The Crimean War brought another boom time and even the First World War pumped plenty of money through the Town. The cost to those who took part was enormous, but to those who survived back in Blighty the tragedies were of a personal, rather than strictly economic nature - apart, of course, from those families who lost their principal breadwinners.

The Second World War, however, dealt Devonport a blow from which it has never been allowed to recover. It was not just pubs that were lost, there were churches, cinemas, theatres and major department stores - and none of them were replaced. The heart was ripped out of the community and row after row of cosy terraced housing was replaced with modern new tower blocks - ideal thought the architects, who never actually had to live in them. There were, of course, those who argued that the economic decline of Devonport was already underway in the 1930s and that, like Stonehouse, in the wake of improved transportation, the centre of attention was gradually being shifted away towards Plymouth itself. However, that does not excuse the shabby way that Devonport was stripped after the war, nor does it excuse the way that the area is being treated today. Clearly the government is putting money into the area but, equally clearly, it is not enough. While the sites of Granby Barracks, Raglan Barracks and now Mount Wise have been increasingly surrendered to civilian use and while there has been substantial funding for the PDC at Mount Wise, does it really come anywhere near the losses that accompany the reduction in the size of the Dockyard workforce and of the Navy itself?

There were over 121,000 naval personnel in the late 1930s, today there are just 38,405, plus 1,958 voluntary reserves, that's barely a third of what it was sixty years ago - small wonder that there isn't support for the pubs here. It's not just the size of the Dockyard workforce that is important for without the ships and without the sailors the amount of disposable cash feeding the money-go-round has simply dried up. The story along Union Street is much the same, although there students have become the new target for many of those hostelries that are left. And it's not just the pubs, it's the newsagents, the pasty shops, the clothing shops and so on ... there simply isn't the money to support them and if the argument here doesn't convince you, take a look around Devonport yourself ... and if you see boarded-up pubs in other parts of the city, remember the Dockyard was the biggest employer in the City by a long way, now it's more or less on a par with the Health Service and the University.

In crude terms then, to appreciate the difference, imagine there were another 10,000 employed somewhere in the City today at a very basic wage of £10,000, that would represent another £100 million pounds a year pumping around the local economy. You need to make an allowance for the money that is paid out in social security, but you also need, in Plymouth's case, to add in all those who might have been in the Navy and you need to take away the revenue from the many more visiting sailors who spent freely here and it certainly adds up to a lot more funding than the city appears to be getting at the moment.

Hence the closed pubs now and those for whom closure is perhaps just around the corner.

PRINCE GEORGE

As is the case with many of the newer licensed premises in Plymouth today, the licence of the Fellowship at King's Tamerton wasn't awarded out of thin air, rather it was transferred, on 16th November 1939, from this once-thriving Chapel Street hostelry just off Stonehouse Bridge. Situated right next to the now long-since demolished Plymouth Brewery building, the Prince George actually predated the brewery by many years. The Brewery was purpose-built here in the early 1890s while the pub dates back at least to 1873. In 1939, just before this picture was taken (note the kerbstones painted for wartime blackout conditions), the pub was closed and adapted as an extension of the brewery.

Today the recently-completed extension to the Marine Projects site occupies the site of both pub and brewery buildings.

PLYMOUTH
P**U**BS
PAST & PRESENT

ARCHER INN

Standing on the corner of Archer Terrace and Essex Street this was just a beerhouse until 1960. That year saw the arrival of Lavinia Martin at the Archer who was to become, quite probably, the longest serving licensee in the hundred years or so that this one-bar ale-house has been trading. Thought to have been built sometime in the 1870s, soon after the completion of Archer Place, a Mrs Granger was an early licensee here in 1880, while throughout the 1890s Henry Benton was in charge of this unassuming beerhouse.

Little changed from that time, there were, until the 1960s, a couple of dormer windows on the front elevation.

Nationally there are dozens of pubs with an archery/arrows related name but this would appear not to be one of them!

PLYMOUTH PUBS PAST & PRESENT

ARK ROYAL

Before the last war the pub at No.5 Fore Street was known as the Devonport Railway Hotel. Interestingly enough, though, it had not always been known as such, the name reflecting a change in circumstances in the neighbourhood, as appealing to travellers on the steam railway was deemed to be a better commercial proposition than appealing to those who cherished associations with Morice Yard, for the old pub was originally known as the Ordnance Arms.

Rechristened when it was rebuilt in the late 1950s, the pub sign had a picture of the 1955 Ark Royal (the fifth) on one side and the original Ark Royal, launched as the Ark Raleigh in Deptford in 1587, on the other side. On 11th June 1997 it was renamed yet again, this time as the Zoo Rooms. After being closed for some time this latest refurbishment has made it look one of the most "modern" of all Plymouth pubs.

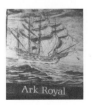

Ark Royal

PLYMOUTH
P**BS
PAST & PRESENT

3

BREAKWATER INN

Nearly 3.5 million tons of stone were used between 1812 and 1844 to form Messrs. Rennie and Whidbey's masterful Breakwater in Plymouth Sound and most of the stone had come from the "quarries on the Catwater".

Hard and thirsty work and so it's no surprise to find that by 1820 an inn had been built on "Cat Down" opposite Fareham Place (which no longer stands and which was doubtless built to house quarry workers).

In the late nineteenth century as the commercial docks expanded, the pubs' clientele changed and in later years, appropriately enough the pub became the Plymouth base for the Mission To Seamen, it also became very well-known as a live music venue.

It was converted for residential use, as six flats, in May 1997.

PLYMOUTH
P BS
PAST & PRESENT

THE BRITANNIA

It was James Thomson (1700-48) who wrote those immortal lines, "Rule, Britannia, Britannia rule the waves" and the Reverend Sydney Smith (1771-1845) who said "What two ideas are more inseparable than Beer and Britannia?"

Certainly there was a local link - it came through the family of Robert Falcon Scott who were living in this area when the original pub here was built. What we see today is very much a pre-war twentieth century mock-Tudor affair ... strangely enough it was in Tudor times that William Camden published his famous survey of the British Isles - "Britannia" taking his title from the Roman, or perhaps even Celtic name for these shores.

Locally the pub these days is famous for being: (a) the closest pub to Home Park and Plymouth Argyle, and (b) for being one of the top live music venues in the area.

PLYMOUTH
PUBS
PAST & PRESENT

BROOK INN

It stands on the Longbrook Street site of what was once Admiral Buller's coachman's house and stables and a fair amount of the material from the old complex has gone into the new. The Brook was built, almost literally, by its first licensee Nigel Hunt - he did his own surveying and most of the electrics. Prior to coming here Nigel and his brother Ashley, his partner in the venture, had an electronics firm in Exeter; this was his first pub. Admiral Sir Alexander Buller died in 1903, his family had been at Earl Hall, to which these premises belonged, for some time, but there had been many others here too. Two hundred years ago there was a family of vintners at Earl Hall - the Langs who later moved to Plymstock. In more recent years the old stables were used as storehouses, shortly before the pub was built, though they burnt down leaving just a shell.

The Brook itself, which runs through St Maurice, is known as Ballam's - or Baldwin's - Brook, after Baldwin de Redvers the medieval lord of St. Maurice.

6

BROWN BEAR

Opened in April 1774 as just "The Bear", it had, in those days, a large bear pit in the cellar which was used for live bear fights. By 1800 it had already become known as the Brown Bear. An advertisement from that year was placed in Woolmer's Gazette, looking for a "Waiter who has long been in that capacity and can bring a certificate for his honesty and attention". For particulars interested parties were to apply to "JA" at the "Brown Bear, Chapel-street" ... "NB - No answer unless letters are post-paid".

Later known, briefly, as the Chapel Street Inn, the pub has done well over the years to survive the many changes in Devonport. Deprived of many of its neighbours during the war, while others have gone since, the Brown Bear has been left a little isolated but in the fortunate position, for an old town pub, of having a reasonably sized car-park. Greatly expanded in recent years, this once small inn is now blessed with a large and accommodating restaurant.

PLYMOUTH
PUBS
PAST & PRESENT

BUTCHERS' ARMS

Time was when each of the Three Towns, Plymouth, Stonehouse and Devonport had a Barrack Street, today, however, there is no such street-name to be found in the city. The Plymouth Barrack Street became the pre-war Russell Street, now buried beneath the buildings to the west of Armada Way between New George Street and Royal Parade, while the Stonehouse Barrack Street was demolished in 1861 to make way for the expansion of the Royal Marine Barracks (from which its name originally came) in 1861. The last to go was the Devonport Barrack Street which was swallowed up in the Dockyard extension of the late 1950s.

It was in the Devonport street of that name, though, that the Butchers' Arms, depicted here, stood. Like the Butchers' Arms in Stonehouse, this pub owed its name to a nearby slaughterhouse which functioned well into the twentieth century. Buckets of blood and freshly skinned hides were a regular and familiar sight just yards from here. Bernard Jackson is the first licensee we have record of here, in 1812, Edna Toleman the last when it closed in the late 1950s.

PLYMOUTH
P◨BS
PAST & PRESENT

CASEY'S

Of all the pub name changes in Plymouth this is perhaps the most logical. For over 50 years the name of the licensee of the Prince Albert in Marlborough Street was William Casey and not surprisingly the pub became better known to all its locals as - Casey's ... and continued to be known as such long after he had gone. Small wonder, therefore, when, some years later, a decision was taken to change the official name so that it matched the one in common usage. Strangely enough though, "The Prince Albert" was not its original name anyway. Rather that name itself dated from some twenty five years after Albert (Queen Victoria's husband) had died. Indeed, in all likelihood, it was William Casey who was responsible for the first renaming of the pub when he arrived here in the 1880s. Prior to that time this was the "Old House At Home" - a seemingly unusual name which is still to be found in other parts of the country. It comes from a once-popular ballad about soldiers wistfully thinking of home while away on service and as such was ideally suited to a garrison town like Devonport.

PLYMOUTH PUBS PAST & PRESENT

THE CHESTER CUP

Time was when there were two Chester Cups in Plymouth, one here in the Stonehouse stretch of Union Street, the other in the long gone Radford Place, just off the old Market Avenue in Plymouth. The latter was a Blitz victim while the former stood until that length of Union Street (between Phoenix Street and Battery Street) was cleared for redevelopment in the 1970s.

Why the Three Towns should have had two pubs named, presumably, after a horse racing trophy contested each May on the 69-acre Roodee Common outside the ancient wall of Chester and close by the River Dee, is unclear. Perhaps there was a big local winner from this area. What we do know, though, is that this was a beerhouse until 1960 when it was granted a full publicans licence and was apparently a Simmonds House when this picture was taken.

PLYMOUTH
P**U**BS
PAST & PRESENT

10

THE CLARENCE

Until the early 1960s it stood on the corner of Clarence Street and Gibbon Street ... its site today lies buried beneath the car park behind the Art College and above Charles Cross Police Station. Like the other Clarences, past and present, in the Three Towns, it owed its name to the former Duke of Clarence, King William IV (1765-1830).

As king he was apparently given to ill-considered public utterances and although known as the sailor king he frequently disobeyed orders and violated disciplinary codes, consequently he was not allowed to command a ship, although he was made Admiral of the Fleet in 1801. Across the country he is commemorated in many pub names, Duke of Clarence, Royal Clarence, Royal Midshipman, Royal Sailor, Royal Tar, Sailor Prince, Nautical William, Royal William, King William and King William IV. This may well have more to do with the time that these pubs were built than his general popularity.

PLYMOUTH
P**U**BS
PAST & PRESENT

CLARENCE HOTEL

Time was when each of the three towns had their own Clarence, each one of them named after the prince who became the popular "Sailor King" - William IV, the Duke of Clarence. Now only this early 19th century Stonehouse hostelry, on the corner of Manor Street and Clarence Place bears that name, even the Royal Clarence in Albert Road has been re-named (see Pheasant Plucker's Arms). Parallel to Clarence Place of course is Adelaide Street, named in honour of William's Queen, by whom he had two children who died in infancy. Consequently he was succeeded by his niece, Victoria, rather than any of the ten or so children he had by the actress, Mrs Jordan, with whom he lived for over twenty years before getting married.

Originally the door to this pub was right on the corner facing the roundabout here, but it was moved some years ago when a Triumph Herald crashed into the building, pinning a customer to the far wall.

THE CLIPPER

Known as the Sydenham Arms for the first hundred years or so of its existence, the pub was run by an A. Sydenham in 1877. As the first recorded licensee here, it is tempting to think that the pub was named in his honour, but the Sydenham name is a significant one locally - Elizabeth Sydenham was Sir Francis Drake's second wife and Humphrey Sydenham was one of the younger officers in the fleet that beat the Armada, so there are other possibilities. Whatever the reason for the name, two sets of coats of arms formerly hung outside this Union Street hostelry - until one of them fell off dramatically, but without injuring anyone, one Saturday morning.

The name was changed back in 1983 when the brewery sank a lot of money into the refurbishment of what is now a free house. Fitted out like a ship in the alterations, the name was changed to the Clipper (the fastest type of sailing ship) at the suggestion of Jeff Luckie who succeeded his father at this popular matelot's haunt four years later, in 1987.

PLYMOUTH
P**U**BS
PAST & PRESENT

13

COMMERCIAL INN

It was the advent of the railways that gave the commercial traveller a fresh lease of life, indeed the term only passed into common usage around 1855. Before long, though, there were small hotels and inns specifically touting for the newly generated custom. By the middle of last century Devonport had a couple of "Commercials", Stonehouse had one and Plymouth had three or four. Today the only one to survive, nominally at least, is the Commercial on Lambhay Hill, and survive it has done against the odds as most of the buildings around it have been pulled down and redeveloped.

A beerhouse until 1953, in that year it acquired the license from the old Newport Inn in Edinburgh Road, Devonport, when that hostelry became a casualty of the 1950s extension of South Yard.

PLYMOUTH
P■BS
PAST & PRESENT

14

THE CORNER HOUSE

It opened over thirty years ago as the Barley Sheaf with the licence from the former, and then comparatively recently demolished, Barley Sheaf in King Street. The site of the original Barley Sheaf is somewhere behind the shops just beyond the point where the present day Raleigh Street meets New George Street, some fifty metres or so from its modern replacement.

The name Barley Sheaf occurs quite frequently around country and like its counterpart Barley Mow (mow = stack) is essentially one of the most basic of all pub signs, simply indicating that "beer is sold here" - barley being one of the principal ingredients. There was another Barley Sheaf locally in Devonport, but that was damaged during the Second World War and was never re-opened.

In 1983 the Barley Sheaf here, however, was renamed, Trader Jack's, in honour of a mythical seafarer. More recently still Trader Jack's has become the Corner House and so, like its near neighbour, The Mall it is currently enjoying its third name in as many decades (*n.b.* more recently The Mall has once more changed its name).

PLYMOUTH
P**U**BS
PAST & PRESENT

15

THE CRITERION

The Criterion stood at No.7 Union Street - the Stonehouse stretch of Union Street, the western end, on the north side, between Brownlow Street and St. Mary Street. It closed for trading on 13th October 1959, brewery man Howard Newnham was listed as its last licensee. Privately owned by licensee Arthur Bowden in 1920, the pub was later acquired by Plymouth Breweries, then based less than fifty yards down the road by Stonehouse Bridge.

James Vosper was the licensee when this picture was taken in the early years of the twentieth century ... the pub name being only just visible in the glass light above the door.

The name itself is not uncommon, in Bournemouth and Weston-super-Mare it is a reference to a pleasure steamer of the same name, elsewhere and probably here it was a name adopted to suggest that here was a standard by which other pubs should be judged.

PLYMOUTH
PUBS
PAST & PRESENT

CROWN HOTEL

When first built the original Crown Hotel, which faced into Cumberland Street and had a 'Tap' in George Street, stood at what was then the main entrance to Plymouth Dock (Devonport). It was one of the most important inns in the town. In 1798 for example, Lord Proby gave a large dinner here to commemorate the Naval victory at Camperdown while in 1799 Vice-Admiral Sir Thomas Paisley threw a grand party to mark his taking command at Plymouth. The Crown was also for a time used as a Regimental Headquarters.

As it stood at the entrance to the town, the Crown was also the logical post house and the proprietor then, Mr. Cowley, had Government Orders to act as a Dispatch Office for the Royal Mail.

In 1880 the Hotel was re-built, as we see it today, with its entrance on the corner of Cumberland Street and Chapel Street. In the golden age of live theatre it became a popular haunt for visiting performers and Harry Lauder and Gracie Fields were among those who stayed here.

Converted to a Berni Inn in 1965 the Crown today, after a recent closure, has just been given a fresh lease of life.

PLYMOUTH **PUBS** PAST & PRESENT

THE DOLPHIN

Probably the least modernised and therefore most pub-like pub on the Barbican is the Dolphin. Drawn and painted by many artists - it's a favourite haunt of Beryl Cook - the Dolphin's main, historical, claim to fame is that an early landlord, Charles Morgan, here entertained four of the six Tolpuddle Martyrs when they arrived back in Plymouth from Australia in March 1838 (after their seven year deportation order had been reduced to four). Morgan was licensee here for over twenty years and throughout its long history the Dolphin has had a succession of long-serving landlords or landladies; indeed the pub is perhaps unique in Plymouth today in that it has stayed in the hands of one family now for over fifty years. The late Betty Holmes pulled her first pint here as a schoolgirl during the war when her grandparents Henry and Louisa Nichols first took on the pub.

PLYMOUTH PUBS PAST & PRESENT

18

FALSTAFF INN

In 1852 this building, then with the address No.1 George Place was operating as lodgings and all neighbouring buildings were residential in one way or another. The Falstaff stood about one hundred yards to the west of Derry's Clock and even less from the original Theatre Royal - hence, no doubt, the theatrical reference in its name ... Sir John Flastaff being one of Shakespeare's best known characters. The preposterously larger than life liar appears in three of the bard's plays and has been commemorated in a number of inn names across the country. There is, of course, a Falstaff still in Plymouth today - in Clittaford Road, Southway, but this one pre-dates it by some time. R.S. Rowe appears to be the one who first converted Robert Ladd's lodgings into an inn, and for over 20 years he ran it as Rowe's Falstaff Inn. His successor in the mid-1880s was also here for over 20 years as were the Grays who followed him. Indeed Emma Gray, who appears to have succeeded her parents in 1922, married Sydney James Perkin and was here until 1941.

PLYMOUTH
PUBS
PAST & PRESENT

FARMER'S HOME

The entrance to the market was on the left, ahead and slightly to the right was, and indeed still is, the back end of Methodist Central Hall. In the foreground just visible is the galvanised roof of Tin Pan Alley which ran up to Old Town Street and Saltash Street on both sides of what was Drake Street.

The name itself was doubtless an attempt by an early licensee to provide a home from home for all the farmers using the market. John Ford, here in 1852, is one of the earliest licensees we have record of but the pub more likely dates from a few decades earlier, soon after the new market was built to the west of Old Town Street in the first decade of the nineteenth century.

Fred Nicholls, here from the early 1880s for the best part of thirty years, was the Farmer's longest serving licensee. Market traders parked their vans here to off-load for both the market and Tin Pan Alley.

FAWN HOTEL

A picture of a four legged Fawn - a seated young deer, buck or a doe of the first year - belies the apparent origin of the naming of this mid-nineteenth century Plymouth hostelry. Standing at the top of Prospect Street, so close to Wellington, Waterloo and Nelson Streets, it is perhaps no surprise to find that the Fawn takes its name from the French 16-gun ship *Faune* which was captured by the British on 15th August 1805. Nelson's success at the Battle of Trafalgar two months later was one of the great naval encounters of the Napoleonic Wars and the *Faune*, subsequently re-christened the *Fawn* was one of the great naval prizes that year. Subsequently added to the Royal Naval fleet, the *Fawn* in turn later captured another great French ship - the *Temeraire*.

William Haywood was one of the early licensees here in the middle of last century, while John Physick appears to have been the longest serving Victorian publican at the Fawn. One hundred years after the capture of the *Faune*, A. Kneebone was licensee here, while the longest serving landlord here so far this century has been Victor Cockram Day. At present the Fawn is a private members club rather than a public house.

PLYMOUTH PUBS
PAST & PRESENT

21

FERRY HOUSE INN

For some six hundred years ferries plied back and forth across the Tamar from Saltash to Saltash Passage and ensured a goodly trade for the inns on both sides of the water. On the night of 23rd October 1961 though, all those years of tradition came to an end, as the last ferry crossing was made here. Licensee Mike Goulding, however, said that the pub would keep its name ... "it will remind people of the good old days". And so it does, nevertheless there is no longer any need now for the A388 sign directing Devon bound traffic to the City Centre along one of the longest roads in Plymouth, Wolseley Road, which runs from here to Milehouse.

Strange to relate, but over almost fifty years before the ferry stopped running the Ferry House changed hands just four times and yet since 1961 it has changed hands on average once every two years.

PLYMOUTH PUBS PAST & PRESENT

FIRST AND LAST

While its external appearance has altered little in a long time, the immediate surroundings have, in some directions, altered considerably, as the First and Last has found itself moved from Laira Road, to Jubilee Place and then to Exeter Street over the last 50 years, all without moving a millimetre.

Located on what was the New Eastern Road, constructed in 1809 to commemorate King George's Jubilee, the First and Last was just that, the first hostelry you saw coming into Plymouth and the last going out.

Built before the neighbouring Church, the landlord here, when St. John's was being erected, in the 1850s, was a man whose initials, strangely enough, were the first and last letters of the alphabet - Zachariah Atwill.

PLYMOUTH
P▯BS
PAST & PRESENT

23

FREDERICK INN

The Frederick Inn was in Frederick Street, part of which still stands today, between Cecil Street and Anstis Street, parallel, appropriately enough, to King Street. The reason for it being appropriate is quite simply that Frederick has been a christian name common to every King George this country has had since 1760; George III was George William Frederick, his son George IV was George Augustus Frederick, while George V (who was born in 1865 around the time that this beerhouse was probably opened) was George Frederick Ernest Albert and George VI was Albert Frederick Arthur George. The name in turn had come from George, husband of Queen Anne (1702-14) who was the second son of King Frederick III of Denmark and thence via her second cousin's grandson, George III's father, Frederick Lewis, Prince of Wales.

Coincidentally the younger of the two boys in this picture is also a Frederick, son of then licensee Archie Colton. The photograph was taken sometime around 1929, just ten years before the pub closed, two months after the outbreak of war.

PLYMOUTH
P■BS
PAST & PRESENT

24

GLOBE HOTEL

When first built the Globe Tavern stood immediately to the south of the original Frankfort Gate and following the demolition of the gate a plaque was erected on the wall of the tavern. Today a plaque still marks the approximate spot - you can see it at first floor level just north of the Herald shop in Armada Way. Around that time the Globe was the last pub in Plymouth on the road out to Stonehouse and Devonport and it sported a sign showing a traveller on horseback "with a Boniface of rotund proportions handing him the stirrup cup with which it was the custom for landlords to bid their guests a safe journey" ... with, underneath, the legend; "Huzza my boys, for Doch-an-dorrach" ... "a whimsical suggestion of the parting drink at the door and an intimation that the traveller was now bound for Dock" (as Devonport was once known). Expanded in 1800 and made into a large hotel, it was pulled down in 1899 and the plum-red brick Prudential Building (complete with plaque) was erected on the Bedford Street site. Badly bombed, nothing now survives of the original Bedford Street.

PLYMOUTH PUBS PAST & PRESENT

25

GOLDEN LION

No.91 Fore Street stood on the northern side of Fore Street, in that stretch between Lambert Street and Tavistock Street. The site is now well within the walls of the extended dockyard and has been since the 1950s, the pub itself, however, was already long gone by that stage, having been a Blitz victim during the Second World War.

There were, incidentally, at one time, two Golden Lions in the Three Towns, the other was in Old Town Street. The name is a popular one in public house history and generally refers heraldically "to Henry I or to the dukes of Northumberland, the Percys" (Dunkling and Wright - Dictionary of Pub Names 1987).

PLYMOUTH
PUBS
PAST & PRESENT

GOOD COMPANIONS

There was a bend in the narrow thoroughfare known as Mill Street, where it curved around to the southeast before almost correcting itself again to run out into Saltash Street. It is on the site of the angle of that bend in Mill Street that in 1969 the Good Companions was built.

A large and rather typical late sixties modern pub the Goodies, as it is popularly known, has, thankfully, so far managed to avoid having its name changed, a fate that has already struck at least two of its city centre contemporaries.

However, in common with so many other town pubs, that is about the only obvious element of continuity here for of its licensees only Ron Shopland and William Hibbert have managed five years here.

PLYMOUTH
P**UBS**
PAST & PRESENT

27

GRANBY CELLARS

It stood on the junction of High Street and Granby Street, across the road from Granby Barracks, visible here to the right. In the early 1960s, the pub, which has been rebuilt since the war, was renamed the Marquis of Granby and today stands boarded up, along with half a dozen or so other Devonport pubs.

The late eighteenth century barracks, and therefore the pub, took its name from one of Britain's more famous soldiers, John Manners Granby (1721-1770). The son of the 3rd Duke of Rutland, Granby entered Parliament at the age of 20, contemporaneously pursuing a military career. He took part in the campaign in Flanders and was present at the great action of Minden during the Seven Years War, 1756 - 1763.

PLYMOUTH PUBS PAST & PRESENT

GRAND DUCHESS

The Duchy in question here was Oldenberg, an historic part of West Germany that was ruled by the Oldenberg family from 1180, when it first became independent, until 1918 when the Grand Duke abdicated in favour of a coalition of Democrat, Social Democrat and Centre parties. Oldenberg in the meantime had, at different times, been annexed to Denmark, France and Germany as the political map of Europe was drawn and redrawn. In the nineteenth century, Marie, the grand duchess of Oldenberg was a regular visitor to Devon and somewhat unusually she was commemorated in the naming of two pubs, The Grand Duchess here in Gibbon Street and The Oldenberg in Paignton (a place she particularly liked).

The picture above shows the Plymouth Breweries house in the early fifties, when it was just a small beerhouse (it received a full publicans licence in 1960) long before it moved into the next-door premises and became the greatly extended place it is today.

PLYMOUTH
PUBS
PAST & PRESENT

THE GYPSY TENT

For over eighty years this unassuming building on the corner of Garden Street and Albert Road traded as a beerhouse - the intriguingly titled Gypsy Tent. Originally Albert Road was known as Navy Row, for obvious enough reasons, in 1866 sailors and dockyardies kept the road in business. Indeed one of the last licensees here served as both - John Martin took the Gypsy Tent after completing his twenty-two-year service in the Navy and, after leaving the pub, spent the rest of his working days in the dockyard.

The old New Victoria Brewery in Hyde Park Road were the last pub owners, they, in turn, had bought it from the erstwhile Devonport and Tiverton Brewery. After its closure in February 1936 the premises became part of the vast St. Aubyn Estate. Before the war Wilfred Palmer appears to have had a shop here and more recently it was part of the Happy Shopper chain.

PLYMOUTH
P**UBS**
PAST & PRESENT

THE HALF MOON

"Tell me but what's the natural cause
Why on a sign no painter draws
The *full* moon ever, but the *half*!"

So wrote one wag many moons ago who was clearly misinformed because in fact there are various moons around the country, hence we have a Moon, a Full Moon, a Blue Moon, a Harbour Moon (Looe), a Harvest Moon, a Moon and Sixpence, and a New Moon to name but a few. By far the most frequently occurring though is the Half Moon. There is one in Falmouth and another here in Pembroke Street, Devonport. Undoubtedly one of the city's older hostelries William Fefher was here in 1798 and Hodkinson, Fawkes, Vallack and Simmonite were among the names of the early nineteenth century licensees who followed him here. The man who doubtless witnessed more Half Moons here than any other though is almost certainly William Brown who was here for 26 years from 1938. In 1997 the Half Moon, like the White Lion in High Street, Stonehouse, was re-launched as a cafe.

PLYMOUTH
PUBS
PAST & PRESENT

31

THE HIMALAYA

The Himalaya stood on the northeastern corner of Stanley Street and Pembroke Street, Devonport and appears to have been rebuilt in 1899. Certainly the architecture suggests that period, but a slightly earlier date would tie-in with the fact that the pub was renamed in 1885, having originally been called the Cornish Arms. Pembroke Street was already in the middle of a built up area in 1812 but the first licensees we have mention of are Richard, then William, Horrell who ran the Cornish Arms from at least 1822 through to 1867. H. Coombes would appear to be the last licensee under that name, while T. Harris is the first under the new name - a name which in all probability came from the great P&O liner *Himalaya* which was launched in 1853 and which soon proved to be far too large for the trade available and was bought by the navy as a transport vessel during the Crimean War.

Strangely enough the pub closed in 1954, 101 years after the sail and steam-powered ship was launched.

PLYMOUTH
P◻BS
PAST & PRESENT

32

KING'S ARMS

A popular pub name - there are more than fifty in London alone - the King's Arms in Devonport is one of three pubs with that name inside the city boundaries. The oldest is at Tamerton Foliot and dates from mid seventeenth century - although clearly not from the time of the Commonwealth under Cromwell when there was no official monarch. The other local King's Arms is at Oreston and is quite probably contemporary with this one despite being architecturally very different. Both are thought to have been built in the early nineteenth century and both have signs depicting the arms of George III who reigned from 1760 to 1820. The Devonport pub - shown here - is even situated in George Street, on the corner of Pembroke Street. Curiously enough the King's Arms in Tamerton is one of at least seven in southwest Devon and Cornwall that stands in the Fore Street of its respective town or village.

A fine building from the outside the pub here is about to be refurbished inside - but one aspect that will remain the same is the gent's toilet which features some of the finest urinals in the city.

PLYMOUTH PUBS PAST & PRESENT

LAIRA INN

Time was when a visit to the Laira might mean a pleasant walk to the outskirts of town. And long had it been that way - the Laira Inn was here some time before the early twentieth-century streets and houses that shape the modern community.

Fishing, lime kilns, its proximity to an early crossing point of the Plym and then the Plymouth and Dartmoor Railway - which ran across the road from this pub - all helped the development of Laira and Crabtree, but it was the arrival of the South Devon Railway in 1848, that really put the area on the map. Thomas Martin was the landlord here around that time, the railway running then, as indeed it does now, to the right of the pub (see picture below).

Demolished in the early 1970s to make way for the road widening here, the Laira Inn stood roughly where you go under the main road, coming into town from Marsh Mills, to head off towards Mutley.

PLYMOUTH
P⬛BS
PAST & PRESENT

LION & COLUMN

One of the most, if not the most popular creature in pub nomenclature is the lion. Britain is full of Red Lions, Golden Lions, White Lions (the one in Stonehouse, however, is now a cafe) and many other coloured lions.

There are also a great number of Lion and whatever; often the whatevers are other animals as in Lion and Dragon, Lamb, Pheasant, Snake, Swan and Unicorn. In other cases they are inanimate objects, as in Lion and Bell, Castle, Fiddle and Key. Generally they refer to some heraldic device, usually associated with the coat of arms of a local family - here at Ham Green however we have one of the city's newer pubs with a name that appears unique in British pub circles - the Lion and Column. Listed in Leslie Dunkling and Gordon Wright's "Dictionary of Pub Names", the name is explained thus - "A heraldic reference to the arms of the Column family, members of which are associated with the local brewery".

Bang goes the notion that maybe it had something to do with Nelson's Column and the Lions that sit at its base - or does it - who are the Column family? There was evidently a lion and column in the bar for some years, perhaps a legacy of Stanley Pope - the first licensee here in 1958 - but BT has no record of any members of the Column family in London or the whole of the South West.

PLYMOUTH
P■BS
PAST & PRESENT

35

LOCKYER TAVERN

Originally built as a private residence, the building that became the Lockyer Tavern was the home of Sir George McGrath, a clever but evidently eccentric physician. He died in 1857 and in the years that followed, his house became Harvey's Hotel.

Not long after this the front garden, which once sported a fountain, was developed and the Wiltshire and Dorset Bank was built onto the front of the premises. This was around the time that Derry's Clock was erected and the whole area became much busier than it ever had been. Lockyer Street itself was developed after the building of the original Theatre Royal, which was championed by the then Mayor of Plymouth, Edmund Lockyer. Ironically it was not long after the building of the second Theatre Royal, in 1982, that the decision was taken to pull down the Lockyer and convert the old bank building into a pub - the license from the Lockyer being transferred to the new hostelry.

PLYMOUTH
PUBS
PAST & PRESENT

LORD BERESFORD

It stands in Cumberland Street, Devonport, and has done for a good two hundred years, but only for the last hundred as the Lord Beresford. Prior to that date it was known as the Black Horse, under which name it can be traced back at least as far as 1798, when John Edwards was the licensee.

There is some confusion in the early part of the nineteenth century, however, with a pub called the Horse and Groom which is also listed as being in Cumberland Street and which on more than one occasion had the same licensee as the Black Horse - neither appear to be listed at the same time and although it seems unlikely, it could be that between 1812 and 1850 no-one could quite decide which of the two names should apply - but the Black Horse it was before and after the confusion. Quite why it was changed again in 1890 is another mystery, but the most likely candidate for the Lord Beresford in question is 1st Baron Charles William de la Poer Beresford, who entered the navy in 1859 and who was a lord of the Admiralty 1886-88.

PLYMOUTH
P▄BS
PAST & PRESENT

37

LORD HIGH ADMIRAL

Not long after Union Street was first laid out in the 1820s, across the top of Millbay on the northern side of Stonehouse Hill (before that great mound was levelled to almost nothing), a road parallel to it and just a matter of yards to the south, was also constructed. This was East Street, so named because it was the most eastern route out of Stonehouse into Plymouth. The street ended, or rather started, here, with the Lord High Admiral - No.1 East Street. The Lord High Admiral in question apparently being the most celebrated of all English Admirals - Horatio Nelson, whose image appears on the present pub sign. Nelson is the most celebrated person of all when it comes to pub names and not surprisingly, given the area's links with the Navy, the Three Towns had several examples of their own one hundred years ago, when in 1895, when Mrs. Fanny Warden was licensee here.

Today, though, there is but this one, where the reference is somewhat indirect - the current Lord High Admiral of the Navy, incidentally, is Her Majesty the Queen.

PLYMOUTH
P**U**BS
PAST & PRESENT

THE MALL

For the first thirty years or so this post-war city centre pub was known as the Eagle. It sported a sign showing an eagle, as in winged creature, on one side, and a representation of HMS Eagle on the other. As a Christian and an heraldic symbol the eagle has been used as an inn sign since the fifteenth century at least, more recently it has been used (in Ross-on-Wye) in connection with the Eagle that was famous as the first lunar module to take a man onto the surface of the moon. In the naval port of Plymouth though the Eagle in question was the aircraft carrier of 1946 that replaced its predecessor of the same name that was torpedoed in 1942. A pub in Dereham, Norfolk commemorates the same vessel in its sign.

In Plymouth however this particular Eagle was renamed Silks ten years ago, and the name change was accompanied by an unprecedented upholstery attack that left it looking more like a beauty parlour than a pub. Strangely enough in the same year the former Malt and Hops pub in Bristol was rechristened in the same way - there however the reference was said to allude to the Law Courts next door where a Queen's Cousel had the right to wear a silk gown (although the sign had an altogether more graphic image of a female barrister in silk underwear).

More recently still, though, this Plymouth pub has been rechristened again and in 1994 was known as the Mall...by 1997, though, at the time of going to press, a fourth name had gone above the door - it is currently the Pig & Truffle.

39

THE MARITIME

Originally a smallish beerhouse (it was a beerhouse until 1960) on the north side of Southside Street on the Barbican, this old pub is one of many in the city whose name reflects the nautical nature of the area. In the late 1980s it was greatly extended when the brewery took over the former consulate building behind it and effectively gave the pub a new main entrance onto the Parade.

Between 1840 and 1880 there were at least six different licensees (Bartlett, Blake, Matthews, Cottle, Priestly and Flanagan) here, but in the 100 years prior to its extension the Maritime enjoyed a remarkable period of stability. Albert Northcott spent over 40 years here from the 1880s through to the late 1920s and then from 1949 through to 1987 Mabel Roberts served here, jointly with her husband until 1968, then on her own with assistance from her son Archie in later years.

PLYMOUTH
P◨BS
PAST & PRESENT

MARLBOROUGH HOTEL

It stood at the north end and on the east side of Marlborough Street, Devonport, until it was demolished in 1973. Up until the thirties at least the main entrance was on the corner, below the sign. Undamaged in the early bombing raid of July 1940 (when Mr. Slee the butcher was the victim of a direct hit a few doors down) the hotel was damaged during the April 1941 devastation and was apparently closed until 1951.

The pub itself was known as the Artillery Arms prior to the early 1890s and it was perhaps the closing of the Marlborough Inn, further down the street, in the 1870s, that prompted the name change here.

The Marlborough in question, incidentally, is almost certainly the celebrated Duke of Marlborough, John Churchill (1650-1722), ancestor of Sir Winston, who was presented with Blenheim Palace in Oxfordshire, by Queen Anne, in honour of his victory at Blenheim in 1704 in the War of Spanish Succession.

PLYMOUTH
P▪BS
PAST & PRESENT

MASONIC INN

After Union Street and the Barbican the stretch of Devonport Road (formerly Tavistock Road), Stoke, from the Pear Tree (No.7) to the Stopford (No. 172) surely has the highest concentration of pubs of any such area in Plymouth. Seven pubs there are in all, the others being the Indian, the Stoke Inn, the Oddfellows and, almost opposite it, the Blockhouse and next-door but one to that, the Masonic. Built, like the neighbouring Blockhouse in the first half of the nineteenth century, the Masonic was just a beerhouse until 1960. A Free House today, it was for many years in the hands of Starkey, Knight and Ford and has enjoyed a regular succession of licensees over the years. Longest serving licensee this century was Fred Williams who was here from 1942 through to 1958 when Elsie Williams took over the licence. Undoubtedly the longest serving landlord in the pub's history, though, was John Batten who turned in a twenty-five year stint between 1877 and 1902.

PLYMOUTH PUBS PAST & PRESENT

MAYFLOWER HOTEL

Long before the multistorey Mayflower Hotel (now Forte Post House) was built on the Hoe there was the Mayflower Hotel on the Barbican.

Situated just yards from the Mayflower stone, commemorating the departure point of the Pilgrim Fathers on board the Mayflower in 1620, this pub was only known as the Mayflower for twenty years.

For most of its life this Barbican hostelry was in fact the Brunswick, probably the name adopted some time around 1820 when Princess Caroline, the Princess of Wales and daughter of the Duke of Brunswick, was accused of adultery and tried before the House of Lords. The Prince, who had already had one marriage - to widow Mary Fitzherbert - declared void, became King George IV in January 1820, and found that Princess Caroline had enormous popular support across the country...the trial was later abandoned. Most "Brunswicks" date from this time, although some are named after the duke himself, who was killed, fighting for the British, at Waterloo in 1815.

Destroyed during the last war, the site of the Mayflower stood vacant for some years before a modern restaurant was built here.

PLYMOUTH
P**U**BS
PAST & PRESENT

MAYFLOWER INN

Like its near neighbour, the Bull and Bush, the Mayflower, in Lakeside Drive, Ernesettle, was opened in 1958. Whereas the other went for an appropriately puny name ("Bull and Bush" - Bush Radio) this one was named in honour of one of the most famous ships ever to call in at Plymouth, the Mayflower, which visited the port in the first week of September 1620.

Although that was nearly 380 years ago it is only in the last 80 years that any pub or hotel appears to have adopted that name locally. In the early 1920s the erstwhile Brunswick on the Barbican, overlooking the Mayflower Steps, was re-christened the Mayflower. However, it didn't survive the war.

Then came this pub, then the hotel on the Hoe and then, more recently, another Barbican pub was renamed in honour of those who sailed upon the Mayflower, the Pilgrims. The popularity of such names therefore appears to coincide with improved travel and communications, making people all the more aware of the significance of those long-distance events. Indeed, the Mayflower Memorial, itself on the Barbican, only dates from the 1930s, although there is an earlier commemorative stone - but even that only dates from 1891.

PLYMOUTH
P**U**BS
PAST & PRESENT

MECHANICS' ARMS

Standing on the corner of the former George Street, now Stonehouse Street, and St. Mary Street, is the corner-house pub known as the Mechanics' Arms. Directly opposite it, in an easterly direction, at No.1 East Street, is the similarly styled Lord High Admiral. Both pubs date from the nineteenth century but while one is named after the great naval hero, Horatio Nelson, the other is nominally more a by-product of the Industrial Revolution and the need for people to have more in the way of education to equip themselves for the new age.

Mechanics' Institutes were essentially an early form of adult education and date generally from the 1820s and 30s.

Extended and fully refurbished in recent years, the Mechanics' nevertheless retains an element of being a traditional pub, something that is becoming increasingly rare in the Union Street area.

PLYMOUTH
P**U**BS
PAST & PRESENT

MELBOURNE INN

It stands on the corner of Wyndham Street and Cecil Street, just around the corner from Melbourne Street and it was built in the early part of the second half of the nineteenth century. Like the street it is probably named after the 3rd Viscount Melbourne, The Rt. Hon., The Hon. Sir William Lamb, Bt. who was born (of disputed paternity) in Melbourne House, Piccadilly, London in 1779 and who died in November 1848. Between 1834 and 1841, Melbourne served three terms as Britain's Prime Minister and it is he who is credited with teaching statecraft to the young Queen Victoria. Melbourne in Australia was also named after him - it had earlier been known as Dootigala. Separated after nineteen years marriage, Melbourne's wife, Lady Caroline Ponsonby, was famous for writing novels and having an affair with Lord Byron.

PLYMOUTH PUBS PAST & PRESENT

NEWMARKET HOTEL

At the beginning of the nineteenth century Plymouth had two Market House Inns, one in Butchers Lane and one in Higher Broad Street. The name itself is a common enough one, there was another in Stonehouse and in Devonport, after the construction of the new market, there was built, in the 1850s, the New Market pub (in Barrack Street). Similarly, fifty years earlier, when a market was created in Plymouth, in 1804, a "New Market Hotel" was built close by it.

Here we see part of the frontage of that hotel sometime around the end of the nineteenth century. At that time the pre-war market was thriving but that did not stop cart sellers setting up, here and there, with their own loads of fruit and vegetables. The pitch outside the New Market was for some time occupied by Dora Stone.

The pub was bombed during the war, a new Newmarket was built in the 1950s, close to the site of the new, post-war, Market.

PLYMOUTH
P**U**BS
PAST & PRESENT

THE NEWMARKET

In 1804 a new market was opened behind the western side of Old Town Street and the inappropriately named East Street was cut through the western side of the bottom half of Old Town Street. Market Avenue and Market Place formed the two other perimeters of the roughly triangular-shaped market and later Cornwall Street was developed beyond the junction of East Street and Market Avenue. At the market end of this new street stood the New Market Inn.

150 years later, some fifteen years after the Blitz had laid waste this once thriving area, another new market was built in Plymouth; along its northern perimeter runs a new Cornwall Street and just off this new Cornwall Street we find Market Way. And it is there we find a new "New Market" bar which was licensed by reviving the licence of the older inn. Current visitors to this hostelry, however, may be forgiven for thinking that the pub owes its name to a different tradition. Until recently we would find a turf accountant's in what was formerly the Paddock Bar, it is perhaps of no surprise to find that the sign on this pub has more in common with the Newmarket in Suffolk rather than the one in Plymouth. Home to the governing body of horse racing, the Jockey Club, the first race took place on Newmarket Heath in 1619, in front of James I.

PLYMOUTH PUBS PAST & PRESENT

NICHOLSON'S

Established in 1871, at 49 George Street, Nicholson's was, until it went into voluntary liquidation in 1936, a popular Plymouth haunt, particularly with aspiring young servicemen. A family concern run, in later years by old man Nicholson, crippled since his younger days by a rugby accident, the Wine Stores was very much a male preserve and few women ever passed through its doors.

Its clubroom was "one of the largest in the provinces" while its so-called Sawdust Club was a celebrated local institution. Nicholson's kept bonded stores in New Street on the Barbican where they kept the wines and ports they imported and blended from all over the world. Nicholson's No.22 Port was one of its more famous creations, along with its No.5 Sherry ... which in 1935 would have cost you around 6/- (30p) a bottle.

Before the war and at the time it was blitzed the premises were part of Smart Brothers Furnishing establishment.

PLYMOUTH
P■BS
PAST & PRESENT

NOAH'S ARK

The Noah's Ark is comparatively common as a pub name and Plymouth at one stage had two - the other was on the Barbican.

The popularity of the name is doubtless due to the fact that Noah is not only credited with planting the first vineyard, but he is also said to be the first one to sample its produce, "…And he drank of the wine, and was drunken"(Genesis ix 21).

The pub we see here is the second of that name to have stood on a site in what was once Saltash Street, just where it branched off the top end of Old Town Street. The original ancient hostelry was pulled down in the 1890s and this grand mock-Tudor structure was built in its place. Bombed during the war, it stood roughly in the middle of the eastern end of the modern Cornwall Street - where it curves around the edge of the wall of Methodist Central Hall. It has since been remembered in the construction of one of only six post-war pubs in the City Centre, the Noah's Ark in Courtenay Street.

PLYMOUTH
P🍺BS
PAST & PRESENT

NO NAME INN

Number 61 Richmond Street was unusual, although by no means unique in the Three Towns, in that it was a beerhouse with no name. Most nameless beerhouses were a legacy of that period in the nineteenth century when it was easier to get a licence from the magistrates than it was to get one from the Excise. In 1869 there were 134,000 licensed brewers in England and Wales, today there are barely a couple of hundred who can brew and offer their produce for sale. There are no pubs left in Plymouth today with no name and nationally a few of those survivors from that era have adopted the building number as the name (No.1 or Number One or One Five One or No.20 Vaults, or whatever). It would have been interesting to see if these premises would have similarly been known. Another victim of the redevelopment of the city centre, it closed in 1956. It stood in behind what is now the northwestern corner of Armada Way and Cornwall Street.

PLYMOUTH
PUBS
PAST & PRESENT

51

NO PLACE INN

LICENSEES

1847 **J. Dodd**
1857 **James Vallack**
1864 **J. Dodd**
1867 **Mrs. D. Dodd**
1873 **John Spiers**
1880 **W.H. Symons**
1885 **James Masters**
1895 **James Dodd**
1910 **John Hendra**
1821 **Edward Wadlow**
1921 **John Uren**
1926 **Wilfred Townsend**
1928 **James Rowett**
1929 **George Curtis**
1930 **Charles Nash**
1937 **Charles Messeruy**
1941 **Frederick Philpott**
1944 **Eileen Philpott**
1950 **Edward Coles**
1952 **Ronald Roberts**
1953 **John Darlington**
1962 **Donald Polden**
1971 **Alan Cookson**
1979 **Barry Phillips**
1985 **Michael Smith**
1989 **Michael Walker**
1989 **Paul Stabb**
1993 **Michael Mortimore & John Pengelly**
1994 **David Moore**

With the tower of St. Peter's poking prominently up behind it, here is the No Place Inn. With its address variously given over the years as Noplace, North Place, Stoke Lane, Stoke Hill and Eldad Hill, there was a time when there was a sign outside here bearing the following inscription;

"Where have you been all day?"

"No Place!"

Authorities appear to be divided over which came first, the pub or the place name, but we do know that between 1830 and 1880 local street maps referred to the terrace of houses to the east of here as Noplace. Throughout almost all that time and beyond it, the Dodd family had this pub - they owned it from the 1840s through to the 1920s. Had Brunel got his way there would have been a railway station built at Noplace in the late-1840s and thereafter the history of this area might have been a little different, as it was, however, the station was sited at Millbay. The top picture here dates from the mid-1950s.

PLYMOUTH
P**U**BS
PAST & PRESENT

NORLEY INN

The Norley Inn stood in Ebrington Street, along from the Unity, on a site now buried beneath the eastern side of Charles Cross car park, on what had been the corner of Norley Place.

A beerhouse for most of its life, it was eventually granted a publican's license in 1960.

The pub took its name from the side street it cornered, which in turn came from the neighbouring Norley Street and before that Norley House. The telephone exchange was later built on the site of the original house and it is thought that the site itself was that of the earliest local settlement...that is the first farm in the area, the south "ton" - Sutton - the southernmost settlement of the Walkhampton hundred. A wartime survivor along with the neighbouring butchers, Melicans, and the Ice Cream Bar - Williams, then Perci's - the whole stretch was cleared to make way for the redevelopment in the late 1960s.

OCEAN MAIL

It stood on the corner of Millbay Road and Victoria Place, on the eastern, Plymouth, side of the erstwhile Victoria Place, opposite the end of Phoenix Street. The other side marked the beginning, or the end, of the Stonehouse stretch of Millbay Road.

Standing at an entrance to the Great Western Docks, the Ocean Mail was an apt name for a pub, past which mail would have been brought from the great ocean liners calling at Plymouth in order that transatlantic mail could more speedily be got to London.

The train from Millbay was a much quicker option than to leave it on a boat bound for Portsmouth and Southampton, from where it would await another train journey.

It was in 1849 that the railway first reached Millbay, not long after the docks had opened and it is likely that the pub was also built around this time. C. Hayter, who was certainly here in the early 1860s may well have been the Ocean Mail's first licensee.

PLYMOUTH
P**U**BS
PAST & PRESENT

ODDFELLOWS ARMS

The sign outside depicts the arms of the Oddfellows and is one of many pubs in the country named after the still active Independent Order of Oddfellows, founded in Manchester in the early nineteenth century. A social and benevolent society with branches throughout Britain and in many other countries around the world, the society is said to owe its name to a remark made about the founding members. The Oddfellows Arms locally is to be found in Stoke village in Devonport Road - formerly Tavistock Road. In neighbouring Devonport of course there is also a sign above the Ker Street Social Club which tells us that the building once served as the Oddfellows Hall. That was not its original purpose, however as it started out in 1823 as the Devonport and Stonehouse Classical and Mathematical Subscription School. The Oddfellows in Stoke, meanwhile, although perhaps of a slightly later date, has always been known as the Oddfellows.

**PLYMOUTH
P▪BS
PAST & PRESENT**

THE OLD CHAPEL

Currently closed and standing on the corner of Duke Street and George Street, the "Old Chapel", Devonport, has been used as a place from which to sell wines and spirits, virtually since it was a new chapel.

Largely constructed in 1790, the building was opened as the "New Unitarian Meeting House" in April 1791. That same year three Unitarians were executed after a riot in Birmingham, while Plymouth Dock Commissioner Fanshaw intimated that any Dockyardsmen who attended the new chapel would be dismissed as disloyal subjects.

The chapel struggled, it closed and was sold less than fifteen years after it had opened. By the time Unitarianism was legally tolerated in England, just a few years later in 1813, the chapel was already being used as a wine and spirits store. Another Unitarian chapel, however, was built in Granby Street in 1829.

PLYMOUTH
P▯BS
PAST & PRESENT

THE OLIVE BRANCH

On the corner of Wyndham Street East and Archer Terrace, the Olive Branch was open by 1864 when George Hosking was the licensee here.

The pub was new then, as was the street and the neighbouring Catholic Cathedral, and George was doubtless the Olive Branch's first landlord in what was then a rapidly growing part of town.

It was quite likely George's pub in every sense of the word too, for after his death in the 1880s his widow continued to run the Olive Branch until Thomas Corin acquired this unassuming free-house around the turn of the century. Corin then owned and ran the pub until Mr. and Mrs. Poole bought it in 1944. Given that the Poole's ownership lasted until 1972 it would appear that in 110 years or so the Olive Branch only changed hands three times - quite a record.

One of many local pubs to change its name in recent years, the pub is currently known as The Library as it endeavours to court the growing student market.

PLYMOUTH PUBS PAST & PRESENT

57

PASSAGE HOUSE INN

Standing on the site of the present Passage House Inn at Cattedown was, until its demolition in 1902, this delightful, angular and partially slate hung old building. As you can see the road here led straight down into the water, where it turned into the slipway to receive the ferry from Oreston.

For those living in the South Hams this was the principal route west (until the construction of the Laira Bridge in 1827). There was a turnpike at a site now buried beneath Cattedown roundabout. After that, the road across the Cat Down, as it was long known, gradually became less and less used, and the extensive quarrying of the area, in the early nineteenth century, left the down and the little village of Cattedown, a mere shadow of its former picturesque self. Nevertheless this is one of the oldest inn sites in Plymouth, the original pub, shown here, was thought to have dated from the fifteenth century and doubtless many an interesting tale was told within these walls.

PLYMOUTH
P**U**BS
PAST & PRESENT

THE PENNYCOMEQUICK

"Pennycomequick is a well-known Devonshire place name, originally the name of a farm. The name refers to the farm's profitability, brought about by good soil. It was recorded first in the seventeenth century and has nothing to do with Cornish words such as pen y cwm wic, as some would have us believe."

So say Dunkling and Wright in their Dictionary of Pub Names first published in 1987. Certainly there are a number of theories for the name and Bracken writing in the 1930s was one who subscribed to the "prosperous farm" notion. However, given that the Celtic "Pen y cwm cuig" can be interpreted as "the head of the creek valley" and given that the tidal Stonehouse Creek used to run up here to meet Houndiscombe Brook flowing down from Tor under the bridge (buried now somewhere under the roundabout in all probability), then the Celtic version is perhaps favourite.

Little changed since the 1950s when the top photo was taken, there have been proposals afoot to make significant changes to this area for many years now, but as yet they have come to nothing. Meanwhile, this busy and distinctive Victorian pub looks out on the passing traffic much as it has always done for the last 100 years and more.

PLYMOUTH
P BS
PAST & PRESENT

59

THE PENROSE

One hundred years ago John Northcott was the licensee of this compact and curve-fronted hostelry. The pub was relatively new in those days, the area between North Road and Western Approach having been developed between the late 1850s and the early 1880s. Standing as it does just up from Hastings Terrace in Penrose Street, it's one of a number of pubs in the area that takes its name from the street it is part of. Its longest serving licensee to date appears to be Edwin Pain who was here for sixteen years after his marriage to the previous landlady Mabel Honey. Of the more recent history one of the more interesting episodes took place when Francis (Frank) Cobbledick, who had a signwriting business, Color Ads, in Hastings Street, announced to his wife one night that he thought they should take on the pub. They subsequently ran the pub for eight years until Frank's death. In his time there though he had transformed the insides of the pub by painting artificial windows and picture frames on the pub walls and filling them with wonderful seascapes.

PLYMOUTH
PUBS
PAST & PRESENT

PHEASANT PLUCKERS ARMS

One of the many mid-nineteenth century pubs on what was Navy Row, and what became Albert Road, the re-christened Pheasant Pluckers Arms, is comparatively unusual in that it appears to have had at least three different names before acquiring its latest appellation. In 1852 Jane Trewin was here as licensee of the Falcon Inn and so it appears to have remained until Robert Burt arrived here in the late 1880s. During his, and his son's, tenancy of this place it became known as Burt's Wine and Spirit Vaults and although there seems to be some grounds for thinking that the Falcon name may have at some stage come back, it was as Burt's that it was officially recorded until 1963. Yet another name change saw it become the Royal Clarence, a name that was to survive until April 1993 when the current licensee gave the pub its latest name.

PLYMOUTH
PUBS
PAST & PRESENT

THE PHOENIX

It is situated opposite the stage door of the Palace Theatre (now the Academy) in Phoenix Street, a street that was laid out along from the old Gas Works in the first half of the nineteenth century.

In the heyday of the Theatre it was quite common to see the stars of a show popping in and propping up the bar in full make-up during an interval or between shows. Three people who would have seen most of them were Charles Williams here from 1898-1919, Ernest Tucker licensee from 1920 through to 1959 and Iris Mosey who ran the Phoenix through to the Theatre's first closure in 1965.

Since that time there have been more than 20 different licensees in this public house. Today, looking forward to a fresh lease of life, the Phoenix is establishing a reputation for promoting young musicians and local groups.

PLYMOUTH PUBS PAST & PRESENT

PILGRIMS CAFE BAR

Somewhat unusually when the pub at No.11 The Barbican was expanded a few years ago it adopted the name of the cafe premises next door (now part of the pub). So it was that the former Sir Francis Chichester became the Pilgrim Cafe Bar. Sad, perhaps, when you consider that the celebrated yachtsman started and finished his pioneering solo round the world trip in Plymouth and personally officiated at the reopening ceremony of the pub in December 1967 - just a few months after completing his epic voyage. Such is the sometimes temporary nature of such recognition that the pub in Citadel Road that was re-christened Gypsy Moth IV, in honour of Chichester's yacht, has also now been renamed and is now the comparatively nondescript Yardarm.

In it's earlier incarnation, however, the Sir Francis Chichester was known as the Crown and Anchor. A popular name with retired seamen who go into the licensing trade the crown and anchor is the badge of the Lord High Admiral and the arm insignia of naval petty officers. Quite when the Crown and Anchor was built is somewhat unclear but John Stevens was recorded as licensee here some 200 years ago.

In 1997 after another refurbishment and in an attempt to be 'modern', Pilgrims became "Bar PL One" - a name inspired by its Postcode.

PLYMOUTH
P▪BS
PAST & PRESENT

63

PRINCE OF WALES

Isolated after the war the Prince of Wales stood at No.4 Russell Street, in that stretch between Frankfort Street and Willow Street. Today that site is somewhere behind Top Shop, on the corner of New George Street and Armada Way. Built in the first half of the nineteenth century, George Ryall, who was here in 1844, and who brewed his own beer, is the first licensee we find in the directories.

The pub, like many others in Britain at that time, was almost certainly named after Prince Albert Edward who was born at Buckingham Palace, to Queen Victoria and Prince Albert, on 9 November 1841, and who eventually became King of England (Edward VII) on the death of his mother in January 1901. Devonport and Stonehouse also had contemporary Prince of Wales pubs.

The top photograph was taken in October 1951, the month that the magistrates' suspense certificate was finally served on the pub.

PLYMOUTH
P**U**BS
PAST & PRESENT

QUEEN'S ARMS

There has been a public house on this particular site in Southside Street for hundreds of years, however, it was not always known as the "Queen's Arms" and the present building has only been standing since the mid-1960s.

The earlier structure was devastated during the bombing raids of 1941 and for two decades there was an empty site here.

The name Queen's Arms, meanwhile, would appear to have come into use for the earlier pub sometime around 1860, during Victoria's reign, and prior to that it appears to have been known as the Plymouth Arms. Famous until recently for the unique collection of over 700 china pigs, amassed during the twenty five year period that Winnie Board was licensee here, the pub we see today was built to similar overall dimensions to its predecessor but the old bottle and jug entered from Friars Lane is long gone.

PLYMOUTH
P**U**BS
PAST & PRESENT

65

QUEEN'S DOCK

Built in the middle of the nineteenth century the Queen's Dock, Morice Town, was originally called the Queen Dock and that subtle difference may well be an important clue to the naming of this Charlotte Street pub. Keyham Steamyard, with its new docks, was completed around 1852 and one of the first major contracts undertaken here was to convert the 110-gun, first-rate, wooden-warship Queen, to steam. Thwarted by being called up for duties in the Crimea, the Queen returned to Keyham in 1855 and, on 5 April 1859, was un-docked as an 85-gun screwship. It is quite possible that the men who worked on this project were among the first patrons of this then new pub - hence the name. J Closh, then Elizabeth Job, appear to have been the first licensees here, while one of the more recent was the ex-Argyle and Everton footballer Aiden Maher.

PLYMOUTH PUBS PAST & PRESENT

QUEEN'S HOTEL

Standing on the corner of Edgcumbe Street and Market Street, Stonehouse was, until the end of the 1980s, the old Plymouth Breweries house - the Queen's Hotel. Part of a well-loved and well-remembered block at the western end of Union Street, the Queen's was right next to the old Stonehouse Market and prospered along with it for many years. Here we see it in all its glory, in later years, however, the top two floors were boarded up, as were a number of the lower floor windows. Now everything here has been demolished and the road has been widened, but curiously enough, not for the first time, the original Edgcumbe Street, which was right at the heart of the ancient Stonehouse community, was demolished way back in 1813.

PLYMOUTH
P**■**BS
PAST & PRESENT

67

RAILWAY INN

With the advent of the railways came a widespread outbreak of hotels, inns or taverns built to service or hoping to catch the clientele of the new transport system. Many of these establishments included a reference to the railways in their title (there are more than two hundred varieties across the country). In the Three Towns there were at least three, the Railway Inn, in Albert Road, still there today near Devonport Station, the Railway Hotel, Mutley, now known as the Mutley Tavern, near the former Mutley Station, and the Railway Inn, Stoke, little more than an iron footbridge away from the old King's Road Station where the College of Further Education now is. Known for many years as Mowbray's Railway Inn, it acquired that name from Joseph Mowbray, the former foreman who worked on the railways in Stoke and then decided to run the pub, largely, it would appear for the benefit of the many labourers in the area who were unpopular in the other pubs. The last pub in Plymouth to gain a spirit licence, it was re-christened the Steambridge in the 1980s, sadly today, however, the pub, which has altered little over the years, externally at least, is currently closed.

PLYMOUTH
P▪BS
PAST & PRESENT

RICHMOND INN

The Richmond Inn, it would appear, stood on the northeastern corner of the junction of York Street and Richmond Street, just yards away from Russell Street. The earliest record we have of it is in 1823-24, when John Crimp is listed as the licensee of the Richmond Inn, Richmond Hill.

The whole area around this location was relatively open until 1820, then began a decade when street after street shot up and New Town, as the development became known, came into being.

Prior to that time, Russell Street, running up from and just outside the original Frankfort Gate, was known as Barrack Street - were they barracks for Frank's Fort? Is that what part of the wall is here? It is difficult to answer these questions for this photograph was taken in the late 1880s, when the pub appears to have been semi-derelict.

It was presumably pulled down soon afterwards and this end of York Street, now buried beneath the car park behind the northwestern corner of Armada Way and Cornwall Street, was itself redeveloped.

RISING SUN

In the early years of the nineteenth century the Rising Sun at Marsh Mills was the scene of an annual party "in the ancient cockle borough of Crabtree, where the so-called Mayor of Crabtree received the Great Cockle along with his newly elected corporation."

The upstairs room in the pub where this all took place was known as Crabtree Town Hall.

By 1854 "none cared to carry on the burlesque" and "the drowsy life of a roadside inn, deprived of all the bustle that thronged around it when coaches were and railways were not, has fallen to it."

Some 119 years after that was written, on 1st July 1973, the Rising Sun was renamed the Roundabout, when developments at Marsh Mills guaranteed a new level of neighbourhood bustle.

But only a dozen years or so after that the pub was closed (summer 1986) for the last time and demolished not long afterwards.

PLYMOUTH
P■BS
PAST & PRESENT

ROBIN HOOD INN

This pub ceased trading on 8th January 1961 and a certificate of discontinuance was issued on the last day of that month. An unassuming mid-nineteenth century pub, Plymouth Breweries' Robin Hood stood on the corner of Union Place and St. Mary Street, Stonehouse.

Although historically associated with the middle ages, the name Robin Hood appears to have enjoyed new popularity in the nineteenth century, in the wake of the establishment of the Ancient Order of Foresters in 1834.

Popular in Nottingham, obviously, there are over 100 Robin Hoods around the country and many more pubs with associated names. Locally the Robin Hood night club in New Street appears to predate all its nineteenth century namesakes - there is record of a pub on that site some 300 years ago.

PLYMOUTH
P∎BS
PAST & PRESENT

71

ROSE AND CROWN

It stood in Old Town Street, on the corner of Week Street, on the site between the Royal Bank of Scotland and the Post Office, running north from St. Andrew's Cross. Thought to have been one of the oldest Plymouth pubs, there is a suggestion that it might have dated back to the War of the Roses. Many English inns adopted the name "Rose and Crown" in the aftermath of the marriage of Henry VII to Elizabeth. Twenty-one-year-old Elizabeth was one of Edward IV's four daughters and her marriage with Henry in 1486 brought to an end the civil wars that had been raging up and down the country for thirty years.

Week Street itself, the lane seen behind the solitary figure in the picture below, was first mentioned in 1585. This part of Old Town Street was substantially redeveloped in the late 1890s, although the pub itself was not pulled down until the 1920s. The top photograph dates from Kissell's tenancy in the mid-1890s.

PLYMOUTH
P BS
PAST & PRESENT

ROYAL ADELAIDE

Among those streets running off Clarence Place, Stonehouse, are Adelaide Street Ope and Adelaide Place. Adelaide Street itself runs parallel to Clarence Place and across the two side streets. It is appropriate that these names appear in close proximity, as the name Adelaide honours the wife of the Duke of Clarence. Born Amelia Adelaide Louisa Theresa Caroline she was the eldest daughter of George, Duke of Saxe-Coburg-Meiningen and she married the Duke two years after his mistress, Mrs Jordan, died, in 1818. Adelaide was 26 and the Duke was 53, although the Duke had sired ten children by his mistress his relationship with Adelaide yielded only two daughters both of whom died in infancy.

When her husband became William IV in 1830, Adelaide became Queen. She died in 1849, surviving her husband by twelve years.

The pub appears to date from her lifetime and its longest serving licensee this century is the current landlady Frances Green.

PLYMOUTH
P\BS
PAST & PRESENT

THE ROYAL MARINE

In 1958 one of Plymouth's newer pubs was opened - it was called the Royal Marine. The reason for the naming of the pub was that David Simonds, of Simonds Brewery, had been well treated by the marines when he had been in Plymouth and he thought that "Royal Marine" would be an appropriate name for a city pub. It had first been suggested that it should be called the Chester Cup, because that was the name of the blitzed inn by the old Market in Radford Place, from which the licence for this hostelry was transferred - but it was not to be and it was a Marine Major General who formally opened this Efford pub in 1958. Alfred (Jack) Sorrell, incidentally, was at the Standard Inn, Devonport for fourteen years before spending another twenty-seven years in the trade here.

The comparatively recent name change to the Lifeboat was one of over thirty pub name changes in the last decade or so, however, it was short-lived and the pub is once again known as the Royal Marine.

ROYAL ALBERT HOTEL

The Royal Albert Hotel stood just two doors from the Keppel's Head and the site where it stood is currently occupied by the wider pavement at the bottom of Albert Road and the Complex pub which now incorporates the Keppel's Head.

Built soon after work had begun on the Keyham Steamyard and standing just opposite the Albert Gate entrance, it took its name from the road, which in turn was named after Prince Albert, the Prince Consort.

Interestingly enough, the name is today remembered in the nearby Charlotte Street hostelry, The Albert, which itself is a modern building standing on the site of the former Charlotte Street Ale and Porter House. The Royal Albert Hotel was one of the many Morice Town Blitz victims on the night of 23rd April, 1941 along with the world-famous Royal Sailor's Rest next door.

PLYMOUTH PUBS PAST & PRESENT

75

RUSSELL ARMS

Number 16 Russell Street was the address of this Tivvy-tied beerhouse. It stood on the northern corner of Russell Street and Willow Plot, on the western side of the street, on a site now just covered by a pedestrianised section of Cornwall Street, outside that part of Woolworths that is nearest to Armada Way.

No arms appear on the pub sign, only the black horse of the Starkey, Knight and Ford Brewery; one can only assume that the pub, doubtless like the street itself, took its name from the MP and close colleague of Lord Ebrington (also commemorated in a local street name and pub name), Lord John Russell.

A popular figure in Plymouth and a leading figure in the Reform movement, Russell - a future Prime Minister, 1846-52 and 1865-66, and grandfather of the philosopher Bertrand Russell - was returned as MP for the family borough of Tavistock in 1813. H.B. Serbidge is the first licensee we have record of, here in 1857.

PLYMOUTH
P**U**BS
PAST & PRESENT

SEYMOUR ARMS

Towards the top end of one of the oldest thoroughfares in Plymouth, the still cobbled North Street, we find the Seymour Arms.

This pub stands in what was once known as Seymour Street and was built when Seymour Street was laid out in the middle of the nineteenth century.

The Coat of Arms used as the pub sign here is that of Lord Alcester of the Seymour and indeed the Culme-Seymour family. At one time major landowners in the area, a lot of land was sold off by the Seymour Trustees in the mid-nineteenth century and that land included plots between Seymour Street here and Seymour Road (and Culme Road) in Mannamead. The family motto Foy Pour De Voir - Faith For Duty appears below the heraldic badge.

Penwain, Brees and Dollery were among the early licensees of the Seymour while Richard Solomon, who came here in the 1880s, and was here for over 30 years, has probably been the longest serving landlord here.

PLYMOUTH
PUBS
PAST & PRESENT

SHADES WINE VAULTS

There were two Shades in the Three Towns before the war; one, with reputedly the biggest bar in Devonport, stood opposite York Street School; the other stood here at 11 Queen Street - which ran between King Street and Union Street - Plymouth. Curiously and confusingly enough, for a time in the nineteenth century, there was also a beerhouse at 11 Queen Street, Devonport.

The Shades in Plymouth, unlike its namesake in Devonport, which had a full licence, had just a Beer and Wine licence. Its site today is buried beneath the pavement outside the Britannia Building Society on the northwestern edge of Derry's Cross.

While No.10 next door was bombed, this Shades survived the Blitz and the Plymouth Breweries house remained open until 1947.

PLYMOUTH
P✦BS
PAST & PRESENT

SHAKESPEARE HOTEL

In 1762, to meet the increasing demand for an entertainment emporium in the expanding town of Dock, a theatre was opened in Cumberland Gardens, its name - the Dock Theatre. It was clearly a lively place and was described in one late eighteenth century account as "a nightly scene of riot and debauchery, notwithstanding the presence of the Magistrates, who use their privilege of admission not only for themselves, but also for their friends."

So popular was it that people came from Plymouth to frequent it, although it derived its support "chiefly from the army and navy."

Comedians were popular here as were Shakespearean cameos and from 1808 at least, the neighbouring Shakespeare Hotel in Theatre Ope was there to serve patrons.

By the late 1890s, however, the theatre itself had degenerated badly and in 1899 it was closed, then demolished and its site cleared. The Shakespeare, meanwhile, stands as a reminder of that long-lost era.

PLYMOUTH
P🕮BS
PAST & PRESENT

SIR FRANCIS CHICHESTER

For the best part of two hundred or more years 11 Southside Quay was known as the Crown and Anchor, a name with obvious naval connections (it is the badge of the Lord High Admiral as well as that of RN petty officers) it was long popular with retired seamen who went into the licensing trade. In 1967, however, the pub was renamed after a seaman of a very different kind, Sir Francis Chichester, who in May of that year had become the first Englishman to circumnavigate the world single-handed. He was later knighted by Queen Elizabeth II, using the same sword that Elizabeth I used to confer the same honour upon Devon's first circumnavigator, Francis Drake.

Chichester himself was present at the renaming ceremony, along with the then mayor of Plymouth (a position that Drake himself once held). Sadly, Chichester, the great adventurer (in 1929 in a DeHavilland Gypsy Moth he became only the second person to fly solo to Australia), died in 1972 and eighteen years later when the pub was redeveloped, and extended into the next-door café, the name was dropped in favour of the café name - Pilgrims (which is now Bar PL One).

PLYMOUTH
P◩BS
PAST & PRESENT

SIRIUS FRIGATE

It stood towards the James Street end of the original Pembroke Street, near the junction with the long gone Canterbury Street. Its address was 16 Pembroke Street and was one of at least two pubs in the street to be named in this fashion (there was also a Phaeton Frigate in the first half of the nineteenth century).

The Sirius appears to have been named after the last warship to have been built by Tyson and Blake at Bursledon, just below Southampton. Launched on 11th September 1813, this Sirius replaced an earlier craft of the same name which was destroyed in 1810, in Mauritius, to avoid being captured. The Bursledon Sirius saw service through to 1860 and was eventually broken up in 1863, its fifty-year history seemingly corresponding with the life of the Pembroke Street pub itself, which was trading under the sign Sirius Frigate from the 1820s through to the mid-1870s.

There have, incidentally, been other HMS Sirius ships at sea since – a wartime cruiser, which was broken up in 1956 and more recently the Leander Class Sirius, one of the Royal Navy's last ever steam-powered frigates - launched in 1966, it was decommissioned in 1993 and used for target practice three years later.

Meanwhile in the 1870s, the pub changed its name back to the Royal Sovereign - a name it first had in the late eighteenth century.

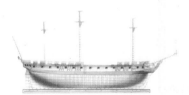

PLYMOUTH PUBS PAST & PRESENT

ST. AUBYN WINE AND SPIRIT VAULTS

Knowing that Plymouth is made up of what used to be three separate towns and a number of villages it is no great surprise to find one or two pub names being duplicated over the years.

However, what is surprising is to find two pubs with the same name not just in the same town but in the same street! However, that is the situation that existed in St. Aubyn Street for some time, until one of them closed in 1935. The two pubs in question were the St. Aubyn Vaults (although one - shown here - appears to have been more properly called the St. Aubyn Wine and Spirit Vaults). To further add to the confusion there appears at one stage to have also been a St. Aubyn Arms in Navy Row (Albert Road).

The one which closed in 1935 stood near the corner with Market Street on the eastern side of the street, while the other, the one we see here, stood on the street's western junction with Cumberland Street. Broderick, one of Devonport's great unsung historians, pointed out architectural similarities between this building and the old Wightwick-designed Post Office on the corner of Fore Street and further noted that there was a Wightwick living opposite this pub site in 1844, not long before we find our first reference to this St. Aubyn Vaults. Could it be that he designed it? Whatever the answer it's not there now. In the mid-50s this pub closed its doors for the last time and the licence was last recorded as being in the name of the great local landowner The Hon. John Francis Arthur St. Aubyn.

PLYMOUTH
P■BS
PAST & PRESENT

82

ST. LEVAN INN

The St. Levan Road viaduct, which ran alongside this pub until late 1987, was first opened in May 1890. At that time there were just a few houses on what was originally known as Keyham Lake Road and which was soon to become St. Levan Road. The title "St. Levan" was conferred upon John St. Aubyn, whose family have been the principal landowners here since 1749, in 1887. Six years later, it would appear, the St. Levan Inn first opened its doors. John Millard was the first licensee we have record of and the curious thing about this pub is that up until this decade, and a few other exceptions, most licensees here have tended to stay for quite some time. Notably Richard Clifton and Jean Gratton who between them, except for 1956, held the licence here from 1916 through to 1978.

PLYMOUTH
P**U**BS
PAST & PRESENT

STANDARD INN

Standing at the corner of Queen Street and at the top of Cannon Street, is one of the area's older hostelries and in one of Devonport's oldest streets. Dating from the early-nineteenth and possibly even late-eighteenth century we see here the Standard Inn.

The royal standard depicted on the sign here, though, dates back much further and back to a king rather than a queen.

Edward III was the first English king to introduce the fleur-de-lys on a royal standard and Henry VI apparently the first to have just three fleurs-de-lys in two quarters and three lions in the other two quarters.

Fortunately, the Standard is being refurbished and is about to re-open after being boarded up for some time.

PLYMOUTH
PUBS
PAST & PRESENT

STEAM PACKET INN

"North Corner Quay - there are constantly passage boats sailing for Portsmouth in which a passage may be procured for 10/6d (52p). The master of these vessels may be found at the Cross Oars, Seven Stars or the Portsmouth Hoy public houses."

So ran an account from a local directory of 1812. Fifty years later steamers were still running from here but there were complaints about their irregularity. There were also complaints from the vicar of Mount Zion Chapel and 30 members of his congregation who were knocked off the pontoon into the Hamoaze in 1865. But for all that, until the construction of the bridge (as visible in the top photograph) between the two sections of the dockyard here 100 years later, little changed in this, Devonport's oldest corner. The Steam Packet and the Swan still stand opposite each other as they have done for the best part of 200 years - however time was when there were five pubs on North Corner (Cornwall Beach) and ten or more in North Corner Street (Cornwall Street). The name Steam Packet itself incidentally probably dates from the 1820s when Thomas Tozer was licensee here.

PLYMOUTH PUBS PAST & PRESENT

85

STOKE INN

There has been a Stoke Inn in Stoke for some two hundred years and without significantly moving location its address has been Union Row, Tavistock Road and Devonport Road, each change reflecting a change in emphasis of the traffic usage in front of this pub. Union Row, doubtless, is a legacy of the period that followed the building of the sixteenth century bridge at Millbridge and preceded the construction of Stonehouse Bridge, when Molesworth Road became a principal thoroughfare out of Plymouth. The easiest route off to the west of this road was through Stoke because it avoided the streams that flowed down from the village to the inlet off the northern bank of Stonehouse Creek. During the nineteenth century, as Devonport became increasingly important, so the coach link with Tavistock assumed greater importance, and many travelled this route, rather than through Plymouth, to get to London. Today the new name is more a reflection that this is a main route into and out of Devonport - it also avoids confusion with the other Tavistock Road in Plymouth. The pub itself would appear to have been rebuilt in 1905 when the street was widened. It is remarkable that only one licensee has served here less than nine years since 1893.

PLYMOUTH PUBS PAST & PRESENT

STOKE VAULTS

Thought to be around 200 years old, the Stoke Vaults in Waterloo Street, is one of a number of delightful little hostelries tucked away in the back streets of Stoke. Run by the Chapple family for the large part of last century the pub has changed hands many times this century and only one licensee, John Thomas (1948-1958), has gone into a tenth year here in the last hundred years.

The pub of course takes its name from the area it is in - Stoke -which in turn was the ancient name for this manor.

After the Norman Conquest it was given to Robert de Albermarla - hence Stoches de Albermarla ... Stoke Damerel.

Stoches or stock itself means literally either dairy farm, or when used as a prefix, simply "lands belonging to whoever".

PLYMOUTH
P**U**BS
PAST & PRESENT

87

STONEMASONS ARMS

Another of the many old pubs on the erstwhile Navy Row, Morice Town, the Stonemasons Arms dates from the middle of the nineteenth century when this area was experiencing a boom time in the wake of the developments that came with the creation of Keyham Steamyard. John Martin, then John Smith, were the first two licensees we have record of here and they were followed by Henry Steer. No one appears to have stayed here all that long, however, and it would appear that the pub's longest serving licensee to date came here sometime after the pub had celebrated its first centenary. Albert Weeks came to the Stonemasons in February 1965 and stayed for some twenty-four years, during which time the pub went from being a beerhouse to having a full publicans license. An unusual pub name in this area (although there are a few Masons around), there was one other Stonemasons in mid-Victorian Plymouth and that was in Lower Street, just off Hawker's Avenue at the northern end of Sutton Harbour - no original buildings now survive there.

PLYMOUTH PUBS PAST & PRESENT

THE SWALLOW

For over 170 years it would appear that this strangely-shaped public house has stood here on the corner of North Street and what was originally part of Exeter Street and is now part of Breton Side. In 1823 Alex Ratcliffe was listed as licensee of what was then the Regent. It is thought that at some stage the building was altered to accommodate a third floor and certainly we know that by the time J. Thomas became licensee here in the late 1870s the Regent had expanded into the building next door - it was then listed as Nos. 16 and 17 Exeter Street. In those days old Exeter Street ran down as far as Embankment Road, much as the modern Exeter Street does today, but little of that original part of the street survived the Blitz or the subsequent replanning of this area.

In the mid-1980s the Regent became Aristocats, as an attempt was made to turn the place into a late-licence disco-fun pub. This move involved incorporating part of the old stable-yard into the public bar and the ghost of a man, cudgelled to death many moons ago in the entrance to the stable-yard, has since been seen in the bar.

In December 1990 yet another change took place here when Colin Damp and his partner Peter Hardman arrived here and breathed a fresh lease of life into the pub which they renamed the Swallow.

PLYMOUTH PUBS PAST & PRESENT

89

THE SWAN

One of the oldest pubs in Devonport is undoubtedly the Swan at the bottom of Cornwall Street. Thought to have been named after the 300-ton sloop of the same name that was built in the Dockyard in 1766-67, the pub would have thrived in those early days, for the Torpoint Ferry ran from the obviously named Cornwall Beach here for many years.

At that time this street was known as North Corner Street, for that is exactly where it was in relation to the Dockyard. This was, of course, where most of the people using the ferry - and living in the street - then worked. It was the first part of Devonport to be developed for housing.

In later years, with the building of Morice Yard in the early eighteenth century and then Keyham Yard in the mid-nineteenth century, so the "north corner" of Devonport moved up the river. And yet there was little obvious change here until the 1960s when the bridge connecting Morice Yard and South Yard was constructed right across the foreground of this view.

Closed in 1997 the building is being converted into flats.

PLYMOUTH
P&BS
PAST & PRESENT

TALBOT HOTEL

One of a number Union Street pubs that have been demolished since the war, the Talbot was, for many years, the meeting place of the Plymouth boxing fraternity.

In 1906 the thirty-year-old Harry Jenkins took over the Talbot and for the best part of twenty years was to be largely responsible for the running of the old Cosmopolitan Gymnasium, which in its day, staged some of the biggest boxing bouts ever seen here.

Named, in all probability, after one of Jenkin's predecessors, James Talbot, who first started selling beer here in the early 1860s, and was still here in the late 1880s, the pub was pulled down in the late 1980s, along with most of the old western end of this grand, early nineteenth century thoroughfare. It stood on the corner of St. Mary Street and Union Street and was therefore properly a Stonehouse rather than a Plymouth pub.

PLYMOUTH
P BS
PAST & PRESENT

91

TAMAR INN

The Tamar, it would appear, used to be called the First and Last, a beerhouse that had its name changed in the late 1880s by licensee William Henry Cudlip - whose name can be seen here on the sign.

At that time there were two pubs in Crownhill, the other being the apparently much older, New Inn, which stood approximately where T.C. Rolt Ltd. are today. Neither survived into the twentieth century as, following the building of the new military barracks in the 1890s, both seem to have been pulled down, with only the Tamar being replaced (by the much larger Tamar Hotel).

Owned at one time by former farmer James Pengelly, both pubs were run by family members before their closure.

It stood on the west side of Tavistock Street, Devonport, at the southern, Market Street, end - the site now stands well within the 1950s extension to the South Yard of the Dockyard. Known originally as the Tavistock Inn, it apparently became the Tavistock Hotel sometime around the 1870s.

One of Devonport's oldest hostelries, it met its unfortunate end on 23rd April, 1941 when Haw Haw's prediction that "Devonport's time had come", in the Blitz of Plymouth, was fully realised by enemy bombers. Fore Street, Catherine Street, Marlborough Street, High Street and Queen Street all suffered terrible fates that night.

A Plymouth Breweries house, the Tavistock Hotel's publican's license was removed to the New Park Inn, Camperdown Street sixteen years later, in March 1957.

PLYMOUTH
PUBS
PAST & PRESENT

THISTLE PARK TAVERN

In the middle of the nineteenth century there was a large open field in Coxside known, on account of the proliferation of a certain wild plant, as Thistle Park.

On the edge of it was built the Thistle Park Tavern, preceding Thistle Park Cotts and Thistle Park Road. John Frost was the licensee here in the 1850s, by which time the railway here was already in use.

One hundred years later, you can see from this 1950s photograph, quite clearly, how close the tracks of the Coxside-Dartmoor line ran past the pub.

Today the recently opened spur off Gdynia Way (which was itself constructed along another part of the old railway), runs along this rail route towards the new Barbican car park - across the road from here.

For the last few years the Thistle has been home to the Sutton Brewery and they now produce a dozen different ales, including Sutton Gold, Dartmoor Pride, Eddystone Light and XSB.

PLYMOUTH
P U **BS**
PAST & PRESENT

94

TWO TREES

Three doors away from the Golden Lion, here at No.88 Fore Street, Devonport, was the Two Trees. Our picture shows it as it was back in the 1890s when the horse and wooden cart were still the principal means of road transport.

The earliest record we have of a Two Trees licensee takes us back to the times of the Napoleonic Wars, a very busy and therefore prosperous time in the history of Devonport. Until the Second World War the very business of war itself did bring a certain amount of economic activity to Devonport, however, that last encounter also brought a lot of devastation to the area for the first time and one of the many casualties was the Two Trees.

The last licensee here, Edgar Leest, was also an owner of the pub and there was a brief family involvement with the modern Two Trees (in Union Street) in 1967.

PLYMOUTH
P**U**BS
PAST & PRESENT

THE VALLETORT

Originally a small beerhouse, the Valletort in Claremont Street undoubtedly owes its name to one of the earliest families that we know to be associated with Plymouth.

It takes us back before the Act of Incorporation in 1439. Indeed it is the Valletorts who are thought to have built the castle on the Barbican - the very Castle whose four towers gave the town its crest all those years ago.

Certainly the Castle stood on what had been Valletort land - the family having been major landowners in the area since the beginning of the twelfth century. The Valletorts were "the first to stimulate the fortunes of Plymouth" (Worth).

The pub itself, of course, is much more recent than that, dating originally from the mid-nineteenth century.

PLYMOUTH
PUBS
PAST & PRESENT

WESTERN HOTEL

On this side of the Dockyard wall, the Western is the only real survivor from 19th century Fore Street. Situated near the entrance to the street, close to various former barrack sites, this plot was, in the late eighteenth century, occupied by the Recruiting Officer Inn. The name commemorated the invidious practice whereby a Sergeant would set up office in a tavern and try to induce local men to join the army. This he would do by offering them the "king's shilling".

Unscrupulous practitioners were not beyond dropping a shilling in a pint pot offering it to a potential victim and claiming him when, drink finished, he would take the now visible coin out. Pewter pots with glass bottoms were brought in to counter this nasty behaviour.

By 1812 this pub had become known as the Old Recruiting Sergeant, then in the 1830s it was renamed the Rising Sun. This name saw it through to the 1870s when, following the arrival of the iron horse at King's Road, this pub, with stables at the back, became the London and South Western Railway Tavern.

In 1938, when King's Road Station was still going strong (the College of Further Education now occupies that site), the pub here was renamed again, becoming simply the Western.

PLYMOUTH
P BS
PAST & PRESENT

THE WHITE LION

There are many who still don't realise that this is a pub past rather than present and certainly despite the large café signs it still looks a little like the old pub it was, from the outside at least.

A rare example of a pub becoming a café, it is the retention of the name, particularly the large, second-floor sign that helps create the confusion. Now specialising in breakfasts and home-made meals, and yes they do deliver, the White Lion has been a café now since the end of 1995, the current proprietor, James Hamilton, taking over the business in November 1996.

Once one of a string of pubs along the road that goes from High Street, through Clarence Place here and into King Street, it stands on the corner of Battery Street, opposite the wall of the former Royal Naval Hospital.

PLYMOUTH
P■BS
PAST & PRESENT

THE WHITE SWAN

It stood in that stretch of George Street that ran between Ker Street and Pembroke Street. Along with the shops that were its immediate neighbours it survived the Blitz but not the long-term post-war re-planning of Devonport. Today the site of the White Swan is given over to a wide green belt that lies between the modern - early 1970s - flats and the original pavement of this part of George Street.

The street itself was first laid out in the late 1770s and the first, substantially-built, housing here was mainly occupied by professional men and their families, who moved into what was then very much the fashionable part of the growing town. In 1830 for example we read that the occupant of 68 George Street - later the address of the White Swan - was Daniel Little jnr., a surgeon. Three doors away in No.71 there was another surgeon, doubtless his father or brother, John Little. There were also a number of other surgeons in the street and several solicitors.

By the second half of the nineteenth century the street had changed and there were numerous shops and three or four pubs where previously there had been mainly private houses.

PLYMOUTH

P BS

PAST & PRESENT

WOODLAND FORT INN

The Woodland was opened not long after the completion of Woodland Fort and for over 100 years it took its name from that well-known Palmerston folly. Of all the great, stone-built fortifications constructed around the Three Towns in the 1860s Woodland Fort has probably the best known entrance, standing as it does right on the edge of Crownhill Road. The Woodland itself, although no great distance from it, on the other side of the road and a little way down Butt Park Road, does not have quite such a high profile, but it nevertheless has been one of the fixed points in the Honicknowle community throughout the area's greatest period of growth. When Alfred Eals came here in 1940 Honicknowle was still a village, little more than a few tiny terraces and some scattered housing, by the time he left in the 1950s it had become another busy development area in an expanding city.

PLYMOUTH
P■BS
PAST & PRESENT

YE BUTCHER'S ARMS

It stood on the corner of Granville Street and Tavistock Road, opposite the Central Library and predated that building by many years. On the lower Glanville Street corner was the old School of Art – the original Tech – and hard behind Ye Butcher's Arms was the old slaughterhouse, hence the pub name.

Formerly slate hung on its southern elevation with an ornate lamp once fixed between the first-floor windows, Ye Butcher's Arms appears to have closed some time before 1920. However, the building stood for some years afterwards; it seems to have been partly used as a chip shop in the twenties, with E. Mills the proprietor. Pulled down before the Second World War, along with the other two-storey buildings in this block, a chemist survived further up towards Sherwell Church for a while afterwards.

Today everything but the Sherwell spire has disappeared from this view as the immediate foreground has long since been cleared to form the front of the Technical College, which became the Polytechnic and is now the University.

PLYMOUTH PUBS PAST & PRESENT

INDEX

Dimcalf, Henry 72
Dingle, J.W. 26
Dingle, Richard 33
Dixon, Ashleigh 46
Dixon, Julie 46
Doble, Cyril 17
Doble, Douglas 85
Doble, George 22
Dodd, J. 52
Dodd, James 52
Dodd, Miss. E. 54
Dodd, Mrs. D. 52
Dodd, William 99
Doel, J 1
Doel, James 1
Doidge, H. 78
Dollery, J.H. 77
Donay, Hedley 56
Donnett, Francene 28
Donnett, Robert 28
Dorman, A. 31
Dorrington, Francis 33
Doughty, George 9
Dove, Albert 95
Dower, Alan 73
Down, R. 81
Downey, Richard 16
Downey, Robert 100
Downing, Paul 22
Doyle, James 2
Doyle, John 98
Drower, Mrs. Mary 87
Drower, Thomas 87
Duckham, Mrs. W. 93
Duff, Percy 23, 36
Duffin, William 35
Duggan, George 4
Duignan, Amanda 42
Duignan, Michael 42
Dumelow, Arthur 20
Dunn-Taylor, Frederick 17
Dunn-Taylor, Lilian 17
Durant, R.H. 43
Durrant, Edward 6
Dustin, James 32
Dyer, William 18
Dymond, Thomas 28

Eals, Alfred 100
Earl, David 84
Earl, John 86
Earle, Frederick 79
Eastcott, Mr. 47
Easterbrook, Brian 87
Edgecumbe, Elizabeth 7
Edwards, Benjamin 17
Edwards, David 63, 96
Edwards, Gladys 88
Edwards, John 37
Edwards, Thomas 30
Edwards, Wilfred 88
Edworthy, Bertram 46
Edworthy, J.B. 88
Egbert, William 68
Elford, J. 84
Elford, John 5
Elliott, Charles 70
Elliott, Ernest 41
Elliott, Irene 82
Elliott, Thomas 82
Ellis, Jack 36, 41
Ellis, Kenneth 59
Ellis, William 93
Elsden-Lee, John 17
Elworthy, C. 68
Emmett, R.B. 101
Emrick, C. 60
England, Edwin 68
Ernshaw, Margaret 94
Eunson, Jeremy 61
Evans, John 54, 68, 94
Evans, Mrs. 17
Evans, Mrs. D. 1
Ewens, G. 17
Fairbrother, Malcolm 7
Fairweather, William 100
Farley, G. 38
Farrant, David 35, 62
Farrant, Donald 100
Fawkes, Charles 31
Fearon, Selina 10
Fearon, Wilfred 10
Feeney, Neil 22
Feeny, Amy 67
Fefher, William 31

Fern, Alan 62
Fern, Ivan 61
Ferris, Mary 30
Field, Ivor 3, 33, 68
Field, John 90
Fields, Charles 60
Finch, F. 7
Findlay, Robert 77
Finton, William 7
Firman, Henry 94
Fitzjohn, Michael 27
Fitzpatrick, Hugh 84
Flanagan, Patrick 88
Flanagan, R.J. 40
Fletcher, Frank 84
Folland, WIlliam 14
Ford, Albert 76
Ford, Brian 33
Ford, Cyril 38
Ford, John 20
Foster, Ernest 24
Fox, Alan 26
Freeman, Frederick 13, 37
Freemantle, William 3
Frewin, Alfred 42
Friend, Harold 22
Frost, Harry 82, 97
Frost, Mrs. S. 1
Frost, Roger 14
Frost, W.J. 79
Frost, William 1
Fryer, Barry 96
Fulkingham, Kenneth 36
Fuller, Mrs. 85
Fullock, Richard 5
Gadd, Harold 80
Gain, Rodney 67
Galvin, James 32
Gammon, John 3
Gardener, J. 31
Gardiner, Roy 55
Gardner, William 45
Garton, Geraldine 57
Garton, Robert 57
Garvey, Francis 26
Garvey, Patrick 26
Gaskell-Brown, Peter 7

Marshall, W. 17
Martin, A. 30
Martin, Charles 42
Martin, Frederick 23
Martin, George 41
Martin, Gordon 55
Martin, Harold 82
Martin, J. 46
Martin, James 33, 61, 73
Martin, John 30, 33, 88
Martin, Kenneth 35, 79
Martin, Lavinia 2, 86
Martin, Thomas 34, 90
Martin, Violet 82
Martin, W. 54
Martyn, Judith 74
Mason-Richards, William
   21
Masters, James 52
Matthews, Eliza 40
Matthews, George 12
Matthews, James 26
Matthews, Thomas 8
Maunder, S. 42
Maunder, Samuel 60
May, Frederick 87
May, Joseph 60
May, Wallace 17
Maynard, Mrs. C. 88
McCabe, Bernard 68
McCarthy, John 14, 96
McCartney, Thomas 59
McCombe, Evelyn 87
McDermott, Terence 28
McGarry, Edward
   5, 18, 47
McGarry, Mary 18
McGill, Jeanette 5
McGivern, Daniel 11
McGivern, Mrs. H.E. 11
McGlinchey, William
   53, 85, 88
McGraw, Bryan 97
McIntyre, William
   10, 13, 87, 90
McKenzie, Robert 90
McLaughlin, R.H. 43

McNamara, Alfred 13
McRitchie, Jane 94
McVicar, Robert 74
Meager, Samuel 75
Medland, G. 54
Medlon, W. 8
Meechan, Frank 7
Meiklejohn, J. 62
Meland, G.M. 67
Melia, Dennis 33
Menhenick, E. 29
Messer, Peter 36
Messeruy, Charles 52
Meyler, Dennis 4
Miles, A. 38
Mill, R. 64
Millard, John 83
Miller, David 35
Miller, Frank 29
Miller, G.F. 42
Mills, John 36
Mills, Reginald 88
Mitchell, John 34
Mitchell, Samuel 80
Mitchell, William 80
Moffatt, George 76
Mole, G. 86
Moles, William 101
Molloy, James 43, 97
Monk, Trevor 100
Moody, Reginald 46
Mooney, Albert 59
Mooney, Thomas 62
Moore, Albert 76
Moore, David 52
Moore, George 97
Moore, Walter 34
Moran, Wayne 62
Morby, John 32
Morgan, Charles 18
Morgan, Peter 15
Morgan, Philip 28
Morgan, Robert 41
Morrell, Samuel
   64, 78, 100
Morris, Frederick 17
Morris, I. 62

Morris, J. 62
Morris, Mary 29
Morris, William 21
Mortimore, Jack 12
Mortimore, John 37
Mortimore, Michael 52, 87
Morton, James 17
Moses, Moses 30
Mosey, Iris 62
Mowbray, Celia 68
Mowbray, Joseph 68
Moyse, Raymond 35
Mudge, Mary 21
Mugridge, Horace 53
Mumford, C. 32
Mumford, Raymond 66
Munday, Mrs. Ivy 33
Munn, W. 4
Munnery, Simon 2
Murch, John 51
Murch, Joseph 25
Murch, Joshua 25
Murley, J. 72
Murphy, James 38
Murrin, William 13
Musgrove, C. 101
Naden, Ron 35
Nail, Roger 35
Naish, Nicholas 88
Nakivell, Barbara 90
Nash, Charles 52
Nash, Terrance 28
Nelson, Jean 28
Nelson, John 100
Nesbitt, Shane 9
Netherton, Frederick 4
Netherton, John 45
Nettleton, Charles 32
Newall, John 100
Newcombe, Paul 63
Newnham, Howard
   4, 16, 22, 28,
   34, 71, 100
Newton, Harry 32
Neyle, C.W. 46
Nicholas, Lily 12
Nicholls, Fred 20